# Acquisition and Management
# of
# Apartment Buildings
# and
# Housing Complexes

I

# Acquisition and Management

# of

# Apartment Buildings

# and

# Housing Complexes

By Pierre Mouchette

ISBN-10: 1540896811

ISBN-13: 978-1540896810

Printed in USA

This publication is designed to provide accurate and authoritative information with regard to the subject matter covered. It is sold with the understanding that the publisher is not engaged in rendering legal, accounting, or other professional advice. If legal advice or other expert assistance is required, the services of a competent professional person should be sought. (from a *Declaration of Principles* jointly adopted by a Committee of the American Bar Association and a Committee of Publishers and Associations).

Library of Congress Control Number: LCCN 2017903317
CreateSpace Independent Publishing Platform, North Charleston, SC

This book is dedicated to the real estate investor

who has invested in residential multifamily houses,

and is now ready to graduate to apartment buildings,

and other multifamily housing complexes.


Congratulations, and you made a good choice

when you decided to purchase this book.


Within these pages, you will find all the information that you need

to get your business off to a great start, and to keep the course for success.

Acquisition and Management of
Apartment Buildings and Housing Complexes

# Table of Contents

SECTION 1   GENERAL INFORMATION ...................................................................... 1

   1.0   Why Real Estate Investment? ................................................................ 1

   1.1   The Investment ................................................................................... 1

   1.2   Methodology ...................................................................................... 1

   1.3   Leverage ............................................................................................ 3

   1.4   Rewards ............................................................................................. 3

   1.5   Market Facts ...................................................................................... 4

   1.6   Analyzing the Real Estate Market ......................................................... 4

   1.7   The Competition ................................................................................. 5

   1.8   Purchasing Strategies .......................................................................... 6

   1.9   Advertising (if you do not use a Management Co.) ................................. 6

   1.10   Retention ......................................................................................... 7

   1.11   The Business Plan ............................................................................. 7

   1.12   Property Ownership ........................................................................... 7

   1.13   Seller Financing ................................................................................ 8

   1.14   Due Diligence ................................................................................... 8

   1.15   Books and Records ............................................................................ 9

   1.16   Physical Inspection ........................................................................... 11

   1.17   Title Review ..................................................................................... 13

   1.18   Financing ......................................................................................... 13

   1.19   Seller Motivation .............................................................................. 13

   1.20   Knowledgeable Others ....................................................................... 14

   1.21   Third Party Inspections ..................................................................... 14

   1.22   Property Condition Assessment .......................................................... 14

   1.23   Environmental Site Assessment .......................................................... 15

   1.24   Insurance ......................................................................................... 15

   1.25   Lender Criteria ................................................................................. 15

   1.26   Investment Opportunities .................................................................. 16

   1.27   Value-Added Strategy (improve value) ............................................... 16

   1.28   Ancillary Revenue Strategy ............................................................... 16

   1.29   Goals ............................................................................................... 16

SECTION 2    PROPERTY STABILIZATION AND VALUES................................................ 18

  2.0    Government Rules and Regulations ................................................ 18

  2.1    Good Cause Law (tenant rights) ................................................ 18

  2.2    Resident Qualification ................................................ 18

  2.3    Resident Selection ................................................ 19

  2.4    Tenant Lease ................................................ 19

  2.5    Mold and Mildew ................................................ 21

  2.6    Resident Warning ................................................ 22

  2.7    Terminating a Resident ................................................ 22

  2.8    The Exit and Refund of Deposit ................................................ 22

  2.9    Property Management Software ................................................ 22

SECTION 3    PROPERTY VALUATION ................................................ 24

  3.0    Property Valuation ................................................ 24

  3.1    Valuation Formulas ................................................ 24

SECTION 4    FINANCIAL INVESTMENT MEASUREMENTS ................................................ 27

  4.0    Financial Investment Measurements ................................................ 27

  4.1    Analyzing Similar Properties ................................................ 28

  4.2    Current Unadjusted Basis ................................................ 28

  4.3    Improvement Value and Depreciation ................................................ 28

  4.4    The Value of Money Over Time, or Discounted Cash Flow Analysis ................................................ 29

SECTION 5    COMMERCIAL LOANS ................................................ 30

  5.0    Commercial Loans for Multifamily Housing ................................................ 30

  5.1    Initial Interview ................................................ 30

  5.2    Lender Programs ................................................ 33

  5.3    Loan Documentation ................................................ 34

  5.4    Prequalification ................................................ 36

  5.5    Borrower Submission Package ................................................ 36

  5.6    Lenders Interview ................................................ 36

  5.7    Commitment Letter ................................................ 39

  5.8    Personal Assessment ................................................ 39

SECTION 6    MULTIFAMILY HOUSES ................................................ 40

  6.0    Definition ................................................ 40

  6.1    Purchasing Guidelines ................................................ 40

6.2    Rent Increases .................................................................. 40

6.3    Management .................................................................... 41

6.4    Using Investment Measurements ......................................... 41

SECTION 7    APARTMENT BUILDINGS / COMPLEXES ...................... 42

7.0    Apartment Buildings............................................................ 42

7.1    Building Classifications ....................................................... 42

7.2    Purchasing Guidelines ........................................................ 42

7.3    Rent Increases .................................................................. 42

7.4    Management .................................................................... 43

7.5    Professional Management Company (PMC) ............................ 43

SECTION 8    PROFILE OF A MULTIFAMILY INVESTOR...................... 48

8.0    Your Income .................................................................... 48

8.1    Assumptions .................................................................... 48

8.2    The Steps ........................................................................ 49

8.3    Investor Qualifications ....................................................... 49

8.4    Forms of Property.............................................................. 51

8.5    Taxable Strategies ............................................................ 51

8.6    Alternative Minimum Tax (AMT) .......................................... 52

8.7    Tax Deductions ................................................................ 52

8.8    Property Depreciation ........................................................ 53

8.9    Depreciable Basis ............................................................. 54

8.10   Recaptured Depreciation, and Capital Gains Taxes ................ 54

8.11   Installment Sales for Tax Deferral ...................................... 54

8.12   Installment Sale Payments ................................................ 55

8.13   Installment Sales in 1031 Exchange .................................... 56

SECTION 9    1031 TAX DEFERRED EXCHANGES ........................... 57

9.0    1031 Tax Deferred Exchange............................................... 57

9.1    Common Terminology for 1031 Tax Deferment Properties are:.... 57

9.2    There Are Three Types of Exchanges: .................................. 58

9.3    Accommodators................................................................. 58

9.4    Reasons for using the 1031 Deferred Exchange: .................... 58

9.5    Timeline .......................................................................... 59

9.6    The "Three Property Rule"................................................... 59

9.7    The 200% Rule ........................................................................ 60

9.8    Effect of a 1031 Deferred Exchange on Depreciable Value............ 60

SECTION 10    WEALTH, GOALS AND STRATEGIES ................................ 61

10.0    Wealth................................................................................. 61

10.1    Asset Protection ................................................................... 62

10.2    Family Limited Liability Company (FLLC) .................................. 63

10.3    Family Trusts ....................................................................... 64

10.4    Limited Liability Company (LLC) .............................................. 66

10.5    Charitable Remainder Trusts (CRT) .......................................... 67

SECTION 11    THE HOME OFFICE ................................................... 71

11.0    According to the IRS .............................................................. 71

11.1    Virtual Addresses.................................................................. 71

11.2    Home Set-Up ....................................................................... 72

11.3    Internet ............................................................................... 72

11.4    File Folders .......................................................................... 72

11.5    Standard Property File Labels ................................................. 74

SECTION 12    THE BUSINESS PLAN .............................................. 78

APPENDIX A................................................................................. 87

        SAMPLE FORMS, CHARTS and LETTERS ................................ 87

APPENDIX B................................................................................. 179

        CONSERVATION ................................................................. 180

APPENDIX C................................................................................. 183

        ABBREVIATIONS AND FORMULAS ........................................ 183

        COMMONLY USED WORDS AND PHRASES............................. 183

APPENDIX D................................................................................. 186

        LIFE EXPECTANCY OF KEY BUILDING COMPONENTS .............. 186

APPENDIX E................................................................................. 194

        RESOURCES ...................................................................... 194

# PREFACE

The purpose of *Acquisition and Management of Apartment Buildings and Housing Complexes* is to provide the reader with a clear and concise standard from which they can learn to acquire, operate, manage, sell and create a Multifamily Housing Portfolio, consisting of apartment buildings and housing complexes

This manual may contain general legal and accounting principles and is not meant to be a substitute for consulting your attorney and accountant.  It is to be used as a guide for obtaining the indicated use.

The letters, forms, reports, and leases are for the convenience of the purchasers of this book.  Before using the above, have your legal and accounting professionals verify that they comply with the rules and regulations of your state, county, and city or town.

It is up to you, the investor, to verify that you comply with all governing bodies.

Please take your time to read and apply the guidelines herein.  In doing so, you will not arbitrarily perform a function but truly understand why it is done.

Pierre Mouchette, author

# SECTION 1    GENERAL INFORMATION

## 1.0    Why Real Estate Investment?

Almost all millionaires made their money in Real Estate!  Those that did not either inherited it, or won it by lottery money purchase.  The middle-class family (incomes between $35,000 and $100,000 a year) is shrinking at an alarming rate because of the financial burdens of our times.  In fact, those who classify themselves as members of this dwindling middle class (approximately 47 percent of the U.S. population) are finding that their wages have stagnated and that their chances of reaching greater financial prosperity are seemingly negligible.

*An estimated 50% of the land in the U.S. is owned by the Federal, State, or Local Government.*

- *38% is considered "non-useable"*

- *3% is currently being used for urban living*

- *9% is still available for use*

## 1.1    The Investment

Investing in **MULTIFAMILY HOUSING** is the best investment that you can make.  Why?

- you control your risk

- you can buy it with very little money down

- you can substantially increase the value of the property, and spend very little or no money doing it

- property values tend to increase consistently

- residential income properties have outpaced all other real estate types, delivering the highest average returns for over 30 years

- you can qualify for substantial tax savings

## 1.2    Methodology

Negotiating, whether you realize it or not we are all negotiators.  During the course of a day, we negotiate numerous items at home, to and from work, and at work.  Now, with the knowledge you obtain within these pages about real estate investment, you are going to change your life, and the lives of those whom you cherish.

There are three basic components to any negotiation. They are:

A. <u>Information</u>: Research and gather all information available. Do not speak to anyone, or place any property offers until you **know your market area inside and out.** This **diligence** includes sales comparables, the rental market, underwriting procedures, and more.

   Through knowledge (seller motivation), we can control the result of the situation so that everyone is a winner. Yes, everyone is a winner!

   No one wants to be manipulated or controlled. Through education, we can learn how to make every transaction a win-win situation.

   A great source of information is the Internet. Through the Internet, you can visit many sites such as the U.S. Census Bureau – American Fact Find by County to research the following

   - average advertised residential rents

   - average residential rent

   - housing cost limits

   - affordable housing programs

   - permits issued

   - renter occupied housing

   - housing occupancy and tenure


   *Note: When I say win-win, I mean you are the winner. The opposing party perceives to have been a winner. Remember, every dollar you leave on the table during negotiations is a dollar that makes your investment more vulnerable and less profitable, and ultimately reduces your overall return. Every dollar you leave behind is one more dollar that you will not have for renovation, making repairs, and/or to invest in capital improvements.*


B. <u>Time</u>: Once you have completed your research, and have found a property that meets your requirements, then it is time to make an offer. Ask in writing on the **Purchase Sales Agreement** (PSA) for 30 to 45 days to complete your due diligence (maybe even longer if the property has 75 rental units or more). When the attorneys receive the executed PSA, they will prepare the contract documents for your signature.

C. Power: "The ability to **control** the situation." The number one reason people give-up their power is that they are afraid. Never assume that the other parties in a negotiation know more than you! You are in control, you are the power, the money person. Worst scenario you don't get the property, but (**smile**) there are plenty more out there, and just think of all the valuable experience that you have acquired.

## 1.3 Leverage

Through **leverage**, we are able to **own a lot** by using **Other People's Money** (OPM). This probably happened to you or maybe a friend when they went out to purchase their first home. For example, the home was purchased for $100,000 with a down payment of $5,000. This five percent ($5,000) was leveraged (95% LTV) to obtain the $100,000 home.

Using the above illustration, we now bring **property appreciation** into the picture. Let us say the property has appreciated three percent during the year. That means that you receive an appreciation benefit of ($100,000 x .03) $3,000. Think about that! This means that you have recaptured ($3,000/$5,000) or 60% of your initial investment in the first year.

$$5/3 = 100/x \quad \text{or} \quad 5x = 300 \quad x = 60$$

*Yes, I have simplified the above illustration. However just think.... change the $100,000 to $500,000 or $1,000,000.... Yes, you get the idea!*

## 1.4 Rewards

Some of the rewards that you will obtain through the reading and implantation of this book are:

A. The ability to enjoy more of the material things that life has to offer.

B. The ability to live on tax write-offs.

   a. Income from real estate investing offers several tax advantages such as

   - Leverage – borrowing money to purchase property is a tax-free event that allows you to build wealth through leveraging

   - No FICA – rent from income producing properties (except hotel and motel rentals) are not subject to FICA wage income

- Low tax rate – gain on the sale of property held for more than one year qualifies for a lower capital gain tax rate

C. The ability to save more for the future.

D. The ability to work from home.

E. The ability to retain more of your hard-earned dollars.

F. The ability to have a more than comfortable retirement.

G. And, yes much, much, more!

## 1.5   Market Facts
- People will always need housing.  There is nothing more important than food, water, and shelter.

- As our population continues to grow, the need for housing grows with it.

- Traditionally, the rental housing market houses the age groups from 20 to 29 years old.

- Aging baby boomers are looking to downsize.

- Fifty percent of all immigrants are renters.

## 1.6   Analyzing the Real Estate Market
There are five different types of real estate markets:

A. <u>Premium Market</u>:  A market with high growth, rapid appreciation, and negative cash flow.

- Requires higher down payment to break even.

B. <u>Growth Market</u>:  A market with good growth, a slightly negative cash flow.

- Requires moderate to high down payment.

C. <u>Stable Market</u>:  A market with slower, stable growth that sometimes produces cash flows.

- It still has a potential of a slight negative cash flow.

D. <u>Cash Flow Market</u>:  A market where investors purchase properties primarily for cash flow.

- Very slow appreciation. Requires minimum down payment.

E. <u>Poor Market</u>: A market lacking the economic influences to justify making an investment in the area.

## 1.7   The Competition

A smart investor always knows about the competition. Compile as much information as possible and keep it in a bound file. This file must be reviewed every 3 to 6 months with addendums as required. Some of the information that you should uncover is:

A. Product of each competitor (unit mix, amenities, cleanliness, etc.).

B. How many competitors do you have?

*Note: Do not make a decision to buy, hold, or sell based on emotional factors.*

C. What distribution strategies do they use to promote and position themselves in the marketplace?

D. How much are your competitors charging for their units? Do they charge for utilities or do they have other "add-ons"? Are your services better or worse? In what way?

- What do potential residents like most about your competitors' products and services?

- Are your competitors adjusting to the market or making changes? Are they successful?

- Resident profile, are they the type of residents that you want? Where do they work?

- What factors are most important to potential residents when they select your community? Price? Quality? Service? Easy access?

E. Are there many vacancies or are tenants having a tough time finding a place to live?

F. What are the current trends in regard to vacancy and rents in the market?

G. What are the financial characteristics and capabilities of your target market?

H. What must you do to succeed?

TOWS

From the above criteria, create a **TOWS** chart. This chart (**Threats, Opportunities, Weaknesses, and Strengths**) will allow you to compare at a glance how your property compares to the competition. See Figure 1-1.

## 1.8    Purchasing Strategies

Purchasing properties at the end of a recession or at the beginning of a recovery phase presents the best opportunity for a great purchase (**purchasing right**).

- This strategy does not apply to making a 1031 Deferred Exchange trade due to the time-line imposed by the IRS.

## 1.9    Advertising (if you do not use a Management Co.)

Personal communication is your first line of advertising! Always answer the telephone on the first ring or have your voice mail say "You have reached the office of **YOUR NAME**," then program the automated system to provide the caller with options for continuation of the call.

Experience shows that the most important ingredient in advertising is to be consistent. All advertising must be planned with a specific style or theme to identify it in the public's eye.

Your Field Office:  The on-site **Resident Manager**[1] is your eyes and ears in the field. The Resident Manager must be set-up with

- a telephone answering machine and phone to answer calls when they are not home

- a cable network telephone system connected to the telephone answering machine and their computer

- a computer so that they can access the internet, and the company web site

- a copy machine/fax scanner to receive information from you, and to transmit applications to you

Home Office:  From your Home Office you should update the company's web site as needed, upload forms for the Resident Manager's usage, obtain tenant applications and credit reports, advertise vacancies, and provide brochures and flyers for the Resident Manager's distribution.

---

[1] See (ISBN 13:978 1537526805) The Resident Manager's Handbook for more information.

## 1.10 Retention

Integral to any business is the retention of existing customers. Retaining tenants is easier than obtaining new ones. You must provide your tenants with rents and services that will inspire their loyalty. Review your TOWS Chart!

## 1.11 The Business Plan

In order to succeed in any business, you must plan your goals in advance. In doing so we recommend that, you create a **Business Plan**. The overall *business plan* should be between 10 and 15 pages. This process will force you to objectively commit and self-evaluate the soundness of what is in your minds-eye.

When you complete your Business Plan,[2] provide a copy of it to your attorney and accountant, then review the plan in detail with them.

## 1.12 Property Ownership

We recommend that all purchased property be held under the ownership of a Limited Liability Company. This "**ABC LLC**" will be the owner of your multifamily building, group of buildings, or buildings in close proximity so that the appraised gross value will not be more than ?.? million dollars. Discuss this with important factor with your accountant. The reason for this is

- asset protection

- tax minimization

- maintenance costs

The ABC LLC will provide **capital equity** (earnest money, down payment, reserve money, closing cost, due diligence, inspection, and tests) for the **Multifamily Purchase**. All preliminary documentation such as the Purchase Sale Agreement (PSA) to be inscribed with "Your Name or its Assigns." This will provide time for you to obtain and file for the ABC LLC, in addition to obtaining the State Tax Registration Number, and Federal Employer ID Number before the actual closing.

The ABC LLC is designed to be owned by its' members. We recommend that one active owner be appointed **Asset Manager** and that this person should be the one who is in direct contact with the Resident Manager, or Professional Management Company.

*Note: In a 75/10/15 program, 75% of the purchase price comes in the form of debt from the lender who holds the first lien position secured by the property; 10 percent of the purchase price comes in the form of debt from the seller, who holds a second-lien*

---

[2] See SECTION 12 for more information

*position that is secured by the property; and the remaining 15 percent of the purchase price is provided by you the buyer in the form of equity.*

### 1.13  Seller Financing

The Seller can, and sometimes offers financing of their **For-Sale** property.  Seller financing is addressed here for two reasons:

A. To make you aware of the opportunity of offering **Seller Financing** when selling an owned property, and to;

B. Make you aware of the inherent values of utilizing **Seller Financing** when making a purchase.

   a. The major benefit to the seller when offering **Seller Financing** is

      - creative "**Buyers**" are always looking for seller financing

      - you can sell the property **for more money** (as long as it appraises out)

      - if you offer terms comparable or better than traditional financing with less or no money down, buyers are readily available

      - the purchase note can be structured so that you will receive interest only on the payments that the buyer makes.  (Gives great cash flow)

   b. A common form of debt financing is for the seller to give a second lien for 5 to 10 percent of the total sales price

   c. You pay capital gain taxes only when you receive the principal.  The note should be based on thirty-year amortization with a balloon payment (principal) due in five or ten years

*Note:  Make sure that your attorney leaves you a "window out" within the first 30 days of signing (without penalty) in case there is something substantially wrong with the purchased property.  Due diligence begins once you sign contracts.*

**All cash received at closing is subject to capital gains.**

### 1.14  Due Diligence

This is probably the most important item in *investment property* pursuit.  Part of the due diligence process is to obtain *all information* about the proposed property.  Do not allow your due diligence period to begin until you have received all documentation from the seller.  Generally, due diligence consists of four contingencies.  They are **Books and Records, the Physical Inspection, Title Review, and Financing.**  Besides the aforementioned, this is a perfect time to find out what is motivating the seller to sell.

*Note: Negotiating is part of due diligence! Whatever you discover during due diligence can be used to negotiate the purchase price down. Remember to "Negotiate All The Time."*

Due diligence is also strategy! During the due diligence period, you must identify specific **Threats, Opportunities, Weaknesses, and Strengths** about the subject property, its' current ownership and management. Ultimately, you want to understand value and define all risks and opportunities related to the investment.

> **If your due diligence uncovers problems in the structure, or mechanical and electrical systems, get estimates to correct the problem. These are negotiable items.**

## 1.15  Books and Records

**Books**: Visiting the Town Hall will provide you with a wealth of information.

Assessors' Office: The local tax assessor maintains a list of taxable properties in their municipality. This **Grand List** contains an estimate of the value of all properties.

- Periodic Reassessment: Since most towns do not have the manpower or financial resources to annually reassess each parcel of real property, the statutes require a thorough revaluation every ten (verify for your state, and county) years. Adjustments made during the interim period are based on the best information the local assessor can obtain.

- Field Card: This document contains information on the property such as the land size, its improvements, and methodology of the assessment. The card also contains the volume and page number that the transaction was recorded on. This field card serves as a basis for the start of your research.

  *Note: Your property may be reassessed to a higher value after your purchase, and you will have to pay more taxes on it.*

Land Records: The **Town Clerk** is responsible for maintaining all public records, which include deeds, mortgage deeds, notes, leases, mechanics' liens, and attachments. Each record is stamped with the date and time, and signature of the clerk acknowledging its official receipt, and entry of the document into the public record.

  A. Grantor/Grantee Lists: The Town Clerk maintains lists separate from all other recorded documents containing information on local real estate transactions indexed under the names of the **Grantors and Grantees**. These lists are a chronological compilation of all types of documents received for recording, and makes it easy to trace a specific parcels' chain of title to pinpoint the volume and page number of the transaction.

B. Day Book: because of the lapse of time in recording a document and the town's clerk indexing it in the **Grantor/Grantee Lists**, they are catalogued in a daybook. Always refer to the daybook before going to the **Grantor/Grantee Lists**.

The following is a list of documents that are normally provided to you as the Buyer from the Seller. This list may be augmented depending on the size of the property and the number of housing units contained therein.

- all plans and specifications related to any civil, landscape or site plan for the property

- all entitlement documents and corresponding surveys of any nature

- mitigation agreements with any governmental agency and any traffic studies for the site or surrounding properties

- zoning agreements, permits, approvals, contracts, and/or certificates relating to the development or operation of the property

- phase 1 or phase 2 environmental assessments (ESA) and geotechnical or soil reports

- wetland reports, including any mitigation plan and all correspondence with engineers or governmental agencies in connection with it

- any previous inspection reports and appraisals

- all notes and security instruments affecting the property

- all rental agreements, applications, leases, service contracts, complete and current rent roll, schedule of tenant deposits and additional fees, management agreements, real estate tax documentation, assessments, insurance policies, and operating statements for the past two years, and year to date.

*Note: When reviewing the documentation provided by the Seller you should always base your analysis on the property's current income and expenses rather than on the Sellers proforma (projected) numbers. A proforma income statement provides the potential (not the actual) income and expenses.*

A. Last three-year *loss-run* report from current insurance company.

B. Last 12 months of utility bills.

- names, addresses, and telephone numbers of vendors or contractors used in relation to the property

- a written inventory of all personal property to be conveyed at close of escrow

Employment Trends

The U.S. Bureau of the Census has a valuable report called the **Local Employment Dynamics** (LED). This report will provide you with the following information

- characteristics and geographic distribution of workers and employers in a particular area of town, county, or region of a state

- the labor shed (where workers live) for employers located in a particular geographic area

- the commute shed (workplace destinations) for workers living in a particular area

- how different employment areas compare in terms of industries represented, wages paid, worker demographics and recent employment growth patterns

- the number of jobs within one, three or five miles of a particular location along with the industries found in these areas, the ages of employees, wages paid and whether employment levels are increasing

- the number of workers that live along a transit corridor and work downtown (or some other area along the transit corridor), as well as an indication of worker ages and wage levels

  o whether access to transit is affecting where workers live and work

## 1.16  Physical Inspection

Go through each unit and record as much information as possible so that it will help you make an informed decision.

For Professionally Managed Properties, have the current **Property Manager** accompany you through every unit so that you can ascertain the amount of work that needs to be performed. The property manager should be able to sign-off on the first years proposed budget of repairs to be made. The interest of the property manager and yours should be the same since a budget will have to be drafted and agreed upon.

The following are some of the questions that should be asked of the Property Manager as you walk through the property

- does the building have any building department violations?

- does the building have any code violations?

- are there any pending government agency violations or infractions?

*Note: Homes built between 1960 and 1973 may have aluminum or aluminum alloy wiring. Most lenders will not lend if these materials are present.*

- are there any new local, state, or national code requirements that should be acknowledged?

- what features would make this property more desirable?

- is the building structurally sound?

- does the building meet its design occupancy criteria?

- is the exterior of the building in good repair?

- are the Heating, Ventilation, and Air Conditioning system equipment working properly?

- are there any recommendations for the HVAC system and equipment?

- is the Electrical System in good order?

- are the Electrical Closets in order?

- is the Fire Annunciation System in good operating condition?

- is the elevator and the elevator machine room in good repair?

- is the building sprinkled, and if so is the equipment and apparatus working and in good order?

- are the Men's and Women's Toilet rooms in good repair?

- what is the life of the various Mechanical, Electrical, Plumbing, and Annunciation systems?

- what recommendations would you make?

Utilize the services of a **Property Inspector**[3] to get into crawl and attic spaces, to check the roof, decks, and siding (yes, all of those nasty places that you cannot get into or do not want to). Make sure they inspect the electrical control panel to verify

---

[3] Before you hire the Property Inspector, verify that they will go into the crawl spaces etc. since most inspectors will only comment on what is visible.

sufficient circuit breakers, capacity, spares, and the heating and air conditioning equipment. Obtain the age of major equipment and the life expectancy of it.

***In addition to the above, consider having a termite inspection and an environmental study performed if not required by the lender to reveal any infestation, asbestos, lead-based paint, mold, or underground oil tanks.***

## 1.17  Title Review

Included with the requested records, you should have received a copy of the title report. If not, your attorney will get it for you. Both you and the attorney should be aware of the following

- are there any violations under the covenants, conditions, and restrictions (CC&R)?

- does the legal description on the title report match the legal description on the PSA?

- are there any liens, restrictions, or interest of others (mechanics liens, mortgages, delinquent taxes, etc.) recorded against the property that the seller will need to remove prior to closing?

- are there any easements? Where?

- are there any zoning violations?

## 1.18  Financing

Part of the due diligence period is securing the financing needed to purchase the property. Normally the financing contingency is somewhere between 45-90 days from the effective date depending on the size of the property.

## 1.19  Seller Motivation

Motivation is why the seller is selling, and this is primary for you to uncover. *Understanding motivation is the foundation of strong negotiating.*

A. Do they need to solve a problem?

- Management headaches, divorce, bankruptcy, death, illness, and lawsuits.

B. Have their circumstances changed?

- Retirement, moving, job transfer, increase in taxes.

C. Do they have other opportunities?

- Exchange, business, and stock.

D. Are they price motivated?

- If they get their price they will sell, if not they will not sell.

## 1.20  Knowledgeable Others
Some of the most valuable information that you can obtain can come from the following sources:

- Current on-site Property Manager; ask them for a list of 10 things that they would change to the property to enhance the Net Operating Income (NOI).

- Maintenance staff

- Postal carrier

- Tenants

- Police call-out reports

## 1.21  Third Party Inspections
Property Inspections:  The **Property Condition Assessment** (PCA) and, **Environmental Site Assessment** (ESA) report must be obtained for every property under consideration for purchase.

## 1.22  Property Condition Assessment
The PCA report contains information about the structure of a property and all its components.  This information is critical to evaluating a property and consists of the following components:

- Site, fencing, gates, and parking area

- Foundation, structure, and roofs

- Exterior and interior

- HVAC, electrical, and plumbing

- Safety and compliance

- Current deficiencies and deferred maintenance

A table of **capital reserve requirements** will be included at the end of the PCA report. This is the amount that will be required during the next 5 to 10 years to make applicable repairs.

## 1.23 Environmental Site Assessment

The **Phase I ESA Report** identifies existing or potential environmental contamination liabilities. The examination includes investigating potential soil contamination, groundwater quality, surface water quality; identification of materials possibly containing asbestos; inventory of hazardous substances stored on site; assessment of mold and mildew, checking for the existence of lead in the paint or in the drinking water, and the evaluation of radon reading at the property.

If a determination is made that the property was built on a *dumpsite or contaminated land*, a **Phase II ESA** will be recommended and should be conducted. The Phase II investigation is more detailed.

*Note: To decrease the premium, increase the deductible.*

## 1.24 Insurance

At a minimum insurance, should include

- all insured parties

- multi-peril policy designed specifically for apartments. If you need additional coverage, the insurer can add it through a rider

- property insurance: including fire, lightning, vandalism, windstorm, flood, hail, riot, snow and ice, termite infestation, and lawsuits

- loss of income: if the structure is damaged (or its contents)

- additional costs for supplying temporary residence following a loss

- replacement cost insurance policy, not an actual depreciated value policy

## 1.25 Lender Criteria

Typically, lenders in this marketplace are requiring a DSCR of 1.25 with 25% down (75% LTV). See Lenders Document Chart[4] for a list of documentation typically required by lenders. Only supply information requested by the lender, nothing more.

---

[4] See SECTION 5.1 and 5.2

## 1.26  Investment Opportunities

When reviewing property information to determine if it warrants additional investigation, look to see if there are additional opportunities to **improve value.**

## 1.27  Value-Added Strategy (improve value)

- Increase rents

- Convert excess storage into rentable living space

- Install timers on common area lighting; motion detectors in laundry rooms and storage areas

- Install water saving devices in kitchen sink faucets, water closets, lavatories, and showerheads

- Replace current appliances with energy efficient ones as required

- Convert central heating systems to a Geothermal Heating System, or a Geothermal Heating and Air Conditioning System

- Install a hydronic lawn irrigation system

- Convert domestic hot water to on-demand (tankless) hot water system

- Protest assessed tax valuation to have it lowered

## 1.28  Ancillary Revenue Strategy

- Convert a master-metered property to a sub-metered property

- Add vending services including laundry, pay phones, soft drinks, and candy

- Add dry cleaning services

- Offer exclusive rights to cable TV companies with revenue sharing

- Provide access to building rooftops for cellular companies

## 1.29  Goals

The goal of every investor is to make great investment decisions, obtain above average profits, and have the property produce great cash flows.  The objective of this book is to provide the new investor with clear direction to:

A.  Accumulate real investment property.

- Provide cash flow

- Enjoy property appreciation

B. Preserve the investment property that you have accumulated.

- Enjoy passive income

- Enjoy principal reduction

- Enjoy property appreciation

- Enjoy tax advantages

C. Distribute and build your investment property portfolio, so that you may enjoy financial independence through tax-deferred asset acquisition of capital.

- Enjoy passive income during your retirement years

- Pass-on your portfolio, tax-free to your heirs

Figure 1-1

**Sample:  TOWS Chart**

| TOWS ANALYSIS | | | | |
|---|---|---|---|---|
| | SUBJECT PROPERTY | COMPETITOR 1 | COMPETITOR 2 | COMPETITOR 3 |
| THREATS | | | | |
| OPPORTUNITIES | | | | |
| WEAKNESSES | | | | |
| STRENGTH | | | | |

# SECTION 2    PROPERTY STABILIZATION AND VALUES

## 2.0    Government Rules and Regulations

Every state, city, and town engages their own rules and regulations pertaining to rental housing.  It is up to you as an investor to verify that you are in compliance.  Even if the previous ownership got away with non-compliance, you may be the one to get caught and non-compliance can result in substantial fines.  Areas to be cautious in are

- maximum occupancy for the dwelling units

- qualifications of a family and its members

- inspection by Health Department before re-renting

## 2.1    Good Cause Law (tenant rights)

Connecticut has a **Good Cause Law** [5] (your state may have a different name for it) in which certain tenants are protected from being evicted.  The tenant must seek judicial relief.  Tenants that are protected are

- tenants who live in a building or complex that has at least five dwelling units and are blind or physically disabled (the disability must be expected to last for at least 12 months or be expected to result in death)

- the tenant is 62 years or older

- whose spouse, brother, sister, parent, or grandparent is 62 years of age or older and permanently living in the unit

The Good Cause Law does not prohibit the tenant from

- paying rent

- following the Lease Agreement

## 2.2    Resident Qualification

In order to determine an applicant's qualifications for tenancy you must have them

- read and sign the Application Information form before completing the Rental Application.

---

[5] Legal definition:  Good cause generally means a legally sufficient reason for a court action or ruling.

- the purpose of this form is to provide them with a subliminal message that your Residents are of high quality, that you intend to maintain this standard, and that you will not accept any unlawful goings on, in or out of the Community. This standard is also followed up by copying and verifying their ID

- have the applicants fill out the tenant Rental Application. This application must be filled out in its entirety. All additional occupants must be listed including their relationship to the applicant

- digital photographs must be taken of all applicants and occupants

- a copy of the applicant's driver's license with their name and current address must be made. You will also need a copy of their social security number and other form of ID that collaborates the information on the driver's license

Collection of a non-refundable application fee must be collected at the time of application. This nominal fee covers the cost of obtaining a credit, tenant, and criminal background check. These procedures provide a safeguard for all tenants and management.

## 2.3   Resident Selection

To be in compliance with all governing authorities you must have a **standard** for resident selection. This standard should be comprised of **Financials, Reliability, Stability** and any **other additional criteria** that you have. If your applicant is border-line, you can reduce your risk by asking for a **guarantor**. The guarantor promises to pay the rent if the resident does not. Don't forget to verify the **Guarantor's credit worthiness** (collect a non-refundable application fee).

## 2.4   Tenant Lease

**Tenant Lease Agreements** are like a work of art. They are worth only the cost of the paper they are written on, or they can have an irreplaceable value. When you have a bad tenant, the value of your lease comes into play. At a minimum, your **Lease Agreement** should have

PROPERTY:

- the apartment address and unit number

- description of the rental unit

- damage to landlord's property

- damage to tenant's property

### DATES:

- lease term including start and end date
- delay in delivery date

### TENANT:

- tenant(s) full name
- a list of the residents and their children with full names
- name of guarantor if applicable (guarantor is not a tenant)
- guests
- pets
- utilities (who pays for what)
- antenna and DBS Satellite Dish
- pest control

### RENT:

- rent, additional rent, security deposit, pet deposit etc.
- rent discounts if any, and conditions of the discount
- how rent is to be paid
- how security deposit will be refunded

### ADD-ON's:

- list of special provisions and addendums
- smoke and carbon monoxide detectors
- environmental problems: radon
- environmental problems: mold
- community code
- swimming pool rules and regulations

### SIGNATURES:

- each page to be initialed by each adult resident
- signature of each resident

TERMS:

- use of apartment

## 2.5  Mold and Mildew

Since Mold and Mildew is an ongoing problem nationwide, it must be resolved at the source.  Make sure that your tenants are aware of the following

**Guidelines to Prevent Mold and Mildew**

- Periodically clean and dry the walls and floors around the sink, bathtub, shower, toilets, windows and patio doors using a common household disinfecting cleaner.

- On a regular basis, wipe down and dry areas where moisture accumulates, like countertops, windows, and windowsills.

- Use the pre-installed bathroom fan or alternative ventilation when bathing or showering and allow the fan to run until all excess moisture is vented from the bathroom.

- Use the exhaust fan in your kitchen when cooking or while the dishwasher is running and allow it to run until all excess moisture is vented from the kitchen.

- Ensure that your clothes dryer vent is operating properly, and clean the lint screen after every use.

- When washing clothes in warm or hot water, make sure condensation does not build-up within the washer and dryer closet; if condensation does accumulate, dry with a fan or towel.

- Do not overfill closets or storage areas.  Ventilation is important in these spaces.

- Do not allow damp or moist stacks of clothes or other cloth materials to lie in piles for an extended period.

- Thoroughly dry any spills or pet urine on carpeting.

- Open windows.  Proper ventilation is essential.  If it is not possible to open windows, run the fan or the apartment air-handling unit to circulate fresh air throughout your apartment home.

- In damp or rainy weather conditions, keep windows and doors closed.

- Maintain a temperature between 50 and 80 degrees Fahrenheit at all times.

## 2.6    Resident Warning

Sometimes good residents make mistakes, or things just happen.  Whatever the reason, we give the resident the benefit of doubt the first time with a warning letter.  This letter serves as notice for the resident to get it together or get out!

## 2.7    Terminating a Resident

The Good:  When a resident has abided by the Lease Agreement but the neighbors have complained about them for various reasons:

- Document the complaints in writing from the complaining neighbor.  Inform the offending tenant of the complaints and hope that they comply.  If the issue becomes non-compliant after repeated notification send them a non-renewal letter.

The Bad:  When tenants do not abide by the lease agreement (non-payment of rent, drugs etc.) then it is time to take immediate action

- always start evictions immediately

- you do not make a profit on an eviction

- the tenant has illegally kept possession of your property and is stealing from you

*Never hesitate to serve the resident with the Notice to Quit.  Each step in the eviction process takes time and a bad resident is a bad resident.*

## 2.8    The Exit and Refund of Deposit

Always send the resident a **Leave On A Positive Note** letter and the **Resident Exit Interview** when told that they do not wish to renew their lease.

## 2.9    Property Management Software

Property management software should be selected for ease of use in the day-to-day operations of your property.  You, your Resident Manager and Accountant should be able to navigate easily through the various functions of the software.

- have instant access to all vital tenant information

- easy and quick access to financial information

- easy and quick access to maintenance management

- flexible reporting options

- track resident by last name, unit, account number, or address

- track additional residents

Table 2-1
_____

Software Program Features (minimum requirements)

| Property/Unit Management | Bank Deposits | Work Orders |
|---|---|---|
| Client / Tenant Management | Bank Reconciliation | Job Costs |
| Management Fees | Late Fee Processing | Purchase Orders |
| General Ledger | Past Due Letters | Custom Reports |
| Accounts Receivable | Calendar/Reminders | Reminders |
| Accounts Payable | ACH and Direct Payment | Special Assignments |
| Budgeting | Track Credit Card Transactions and Balances | Complete transaction history for each Resident |
| Inventory | ACH and Direct Payment | Built-in Word processor |
| Vendors | E-mail Capabilities | User Defined Fields |
| Security Management | Attach pictures, files, documents and notes | Download Lockbox transactions |

## SECTION 3    PROPERTY VALUATION

### 3.0    Property Valuation

The three traditional approaches used in valuating and appraising real property are Sales Comparison, Replacement, and Income.

Sales Comparison

This approach is based upon the principal of substitution.  A valuation principal that states that a prudent purchaser would pay no more for real property than the cost of acquiring an equally desirable substitute on the open market.

This method examines like properties and adjusts value based on similarities and differences.

Replacement

The cost approach is based on the premise that the value of a property can be indicated by the current cost to construct a reproduction or replacement for the improvements minus the amount of depreciation, plus the cost of the land and entrepreneurial profit.

The replacement cost is not used to value income-producing properties such as multifamily housing.  It is appropriately used when estimating the actual costs associated with replacing all of the physical assets destroyed by fire, tornado, etc.

Income

The income approach is based on value, and is most applicable to investment properties.  The income capitalization approach is a process of estimating the value of real property based upon the principle that value is directly related to the present value of all future net income attributable to the property.

*Note:  Most insurance companies will include some compensation for loss of income incurred as a direct result of fire (or for any other reasons as stated in your policy).  You must continue to pay all bills on the property during a disaster.*

### 3.1    Valuation Formulas

- Net Operating Income (NOI)

   NOI = Gross Operating Income (GOI) - Operating Expenses (OE)

- The Income Approach uses a property's NOI to determine its value.

Purchase Price = NOI/CAP Rate   (i.e.  NOI=$98,000; CAP Rate=8%; PP=$1,225,000)

- Capitalization Rate (CAP Rate):  A valuation method used to estimate a purchase price.  When Net Operating Income is expected to grow, property trades at a low CAP Rate.

  CAP Rate = NOI/PP   (i.e.  NOI=8%; PP=$1,225,000; CAP Rate=.08)

  To reverse this procedure, i.e. you know the properties in the area are selling with a CAP rate of 8% then, PP=NOI/CAP Rate

- Gross Income Multiplier (GIM):  Is used to calculate the total Purchase Price divided by the Potential Gross Income (PGI)

  GIM = PP/PGI   (i.e.  PP=$1,225,000; PGI=$153,500; GIM=7.98)

- Gross Rent Multiplier (GRM):  Is used to calculate the Market Value (MV) of an income property.

  GRM = MV/Gross Scheduled Income (GSI) or

  MV = GRM x GSI

- Gross Scheduled Income (GSI)

  GSI = total rent payable for occupied spaces + potential rent for vacant spaces.

- Gross Operating Income (GOI) or Effective Gross Income (EGI)

  GOI = GSI - Vacancy and Credit Loss

- Return on Equity (ROE) is expressed as a percentage and is a calculation based on end of first year performance. (*annual formula*)

  ROE = Annual Cash Flow / Initial Cash Input (equity)

- Break Even Ratio (BER) also known as default ratio is a benchmark used by lenders when underwriting commercial mortgages.  Its purpose is to estimate how vulnerable a property is to defaulting on its debt should rental income decline. (*annual formula*)

BER = (Debt Service (DS) + Operating Expenses (OE) / Gross Operating Expenses (GOI)

**Note:  Most lenders look for a BER of 85% or less.**

- Price per Unit (PPU):  Gives the Price Per Unit by dividing the Purchase Price by the Number of Units.

  PPU = PP / Number of Units   (i.e.  PP=$1,225,000; # units=12; PPU=$102,083.33)

- Price per Foot (PPF):  Gives the cost Price Per Foot dividing the Purchase Price by the Rentable Square Feet.

  PPF = PP /RSF (i.e.  PP=$1,225,000; RSF=25,000; PPF=$49.00)

- Cash on Cash Return (CCR) or Equity Dividend Rate is the ratio between the property's cash flow in a particular year (before taxes) and, the amount of initial capital investment. (*annual formula*)

  CCR = Actual Cash Flow (ACF) / Equity

- Rule of 72's

  The Rule of 72's is used to calculate the approximate number of years for an investment to double in value at a particular rate of compound interest.

  Number of years to double in value (illustration uses 8%)

  (Approximate) = 72/rate of growth.  (I.e. 72/8 = 9)

  (Actual) = 72.73/rate of growth (i.e. 72.23/8 = 9.03

**Note:  Never pay full price no matter how good the property looks.  Always make your initial offer 5-10 percent less (seller's buffer) than the asking price.**

# SECTION 4     FINANCIAL INVESTMENT MEASUREMENTS

## 4.0   Financial Investment Measurements

The most effective way to measure Real Estate Investments is to determine the rate of **Return-On-Equity** (ROE). **Cash Flow, Appreciation, Principal Reduction and Tax Advantages** are the four key components to this equation.

- Formula:      Annual Cash Flow / Equity = Cash Flow ROE

A. Cash Flow: The money left after operating and other expenses are deducted from the gross income.

Gross Schedule Income (GSI): The annualized sum total of the current rent roll, and other income such as laundry, vending machines etc.

- Vacancy Allowance and Credit Loss: The period of time when the unit is not earning and/or bank charges for tenants' insufficient funds. Use a factor of 5% unless the subject property indicates a larger percentage.

*Note: If there is no vacancy, then the rents may be too low.*

- Reserves and Replacement: All purchases for real property must include a minimum reserve. This reserve is used to cover any capital improvements to the property. Lenders will often calculate a budgeted amount based on the **Property Condition Assessment Report** to make necessary capital improvements. If the Lender does not give you an amount to be held for Reserves and Replacements, use the following as a guide:

| Number of Units | Or / Per Unit | Minimum Amount |
|:---:|:---:|:---:|
| < 100 | $250.00 | $25,000.00 |
| 101 - 250 | $200.00 | $50,000.00 |
| > 250 | $180.00 | $100,000.00 |

B. Appreciation: the amount that the property increases in value over time due to location, property type, rental rates, and other variables. Two to three percent is a good conservative number to use.

**We use 2.5%. You can verify this percentage with your local Realtor®.**

*Appreciation Return on Equity decreases in time. i.e. The return on investment is not working as hard as it did on the first day you purchased the property.*

C. <u>Principal Reduction</u>:  the amount the principal is reduced by making monthly loan payments.  In the beginning, most of your payment is applied toward interest.  As the loan matures, more of the payment is applied toward principal.

Formula:  ROE on Principal Reduction = Principal Reduction / Equity

D. <u>Tax Advantages</u>:  The amount that you can deduct against your tax liability.

## 4.1    Analyzing Similar Properties

Using the **Annual Property Operating Data Form** (APOD) you can determine how big a bite each expense takes out of your income by computing the percentage of GOI that each expense represents.  You can accomplish this by dividing each expense by the GOI and multiplying the result by 100.

When you compare the individual operating expenses by percentages for similar properties, you can evaluate if your expenses are in synchronization with other investors, or if the individual operating expense should be examined more closely.  Review this with your accountant.

## 4.2    Current Unadjusted Basis

Determine the corresponding value of land and its improvements.  By having this information, you will be able to determine the property's current improvement ratio.  The total value of the property is called the unadjusted basis.  The adjusted basis is used to calculate recovery depreciation and capital gain when the property is sold.

- Example:  The safe way to determine improvements is:

| | | |
|---|---|---|
| Land = | $30,000.00 | 15% |
| Improvements = | $170,000.00 | 85% |
| TOTAL = | $200,000.00 | 100% |

$170,000.00/$200,000.00 = 85%

## 4.3    Improvement Value and Depreciation

From the copy of the field card that you obtained at the Assessors' Office, calculate the percentage for property improvement.  You can then calculate your depreciation basis as follows:

- Purchase Price (PP) x ___% = Improvement Value

- Depreciation = Improvement Value / 27.5

## 4.4   The Value of Money Over Time, or Discounted Cash Flow Analysis

An investment is the present worth of an anticipated future income or, money you receive today is worth more than what you will receive in the future.  To calculate this value, you must calculate the present value of future cash flow.  Present Value (PV) represents the present worth of all future benefits.  (i.e.  If a property cost $80k today and will be worth $95K in 10 years then, the difference between the two values is called Net Present Value (NPV).

## SECTION 5    COMMERCIAL LOANS

### 5.0    Commercial Loans for Multifamily Housing

Banks and Mortgage Companies originate the Small Balance Commercial Loan.  The mortgage is then sold to Investment Banks and Wall Street Conduits.  These banks and conduits then package and sell the mortgages into securitizations.

A.  The problem with a Small Balance Loan is:

- Your personal credit is attached to the investment property.

- If you wish to prepay the loan prior to the end of the loan term, you are locked out.

B.  The benefit of a Small Balance Commercial Loan is:

- It provides a great opportunity to get into the Multifamily Housing market.

- More emphasis is placed on the borrower's personal credit score rather than the asset's performance.

Commercial Loans are investment loans, and the lending requirements are much stricter than Small Balance Commercial Loans.  Because each property is unique, commercial loans are not hard and fast (you can have a borrower with a perfect credit bureau score, but if the property is bad, no bank or investor wants to invest in it).

*Note:  If you use a commercial bank, verify that they have a direct conduit to the commercial secondary market.*

Most commercial lenders look at the COLLATERAL or the appraised value of the property, and the BUSINESS ENTERPRISE or the ability of the business to repay the loan.  In the case of the start-up business where there is no historical track record, the lender will look at the expertise of the borrower(s) and the value of the collateral.  If the lender feels that the borrower has good experience and can provide solid projections based on a sound Business Plan, they may be induced to provide the necessary financing.

### 5.1    Initial Interview

The Mortgage Broker or Bank (Lender) will review different programs with you, the prospective borrower.  During the interview, the Mortgage Lender will ask you to sign an agreement that will allow them to assemble your information, copy files, and complete your credit application.

The Lender's back-office staff will process the application for credit, including the verification of information received, the ordering of vendor reports and the preparation of documentation for submission to the loan commitment. Loan processing is the verification of information given, and the search for missing or unanswered questions and documentation. The processor analyzes both the borrower and the property in relationship to the loan.

Overview of Loan Programs

A. Commercial loans are underwritten on a case-by-case basis. Each application is unique and evaluated on its own merits, although there are some common elements in the basic underwriting requirements.

B. The first step that the Lender must take is to analyze the financial risk of the property. In order to quote you a rate (posted rates are those secured under the best of conditions with no risk), the Lender must determine the following:

- Loan to Value (this ratio seldom exceeds 75% of the fair market value of the property).

- Debt Service Coverage Ratio (most lenders require the DSCR ratio to exceed 1.15. A DSCR of less than 1.0 means that the property does not produce enough income to make mortgage payments).

- Personal Debt Service Coverage (this is the Borrower's Personal Monthly Debt/Monthly Personal Income).

| Borrower: Single Asset Entity | SMALL BALANCE Tier1: Mixed Use; Multifamily Housing | CONVENTIONAL Owner Ocupied or Investor |
|---|---|---|
| **LENDER PROGRAMS** | | |
| Documentation | Standard | Standard, 2 years of historical income required. |
| Loan Documentation | Permanent first mortgage loans for acquisition financing and refinancing. | Permanent first mortgage loans for acquisition financing and refinancing. |
| **LOAN AMOUNT / TERMS** | | |
| Loan Amount | Up to $5,000,000.00 | Up to $25,000,000.00 |

| | | |
|---|---|---|
| Loan Term | 10, 15, 20, 25 or 30-years. Amortization is usually 25 to 30 years. | 10 or 15 years. 15, 20, 25 & 30 years amortization. |
| Pricing | Tiered pricing matrix. More favorable terms available for higher DSC and lower LTV. | Varies |
| Interest Rate | Fixed or Adjustment | Fixed or adjustable. |
| Pre-Payment Penalty | Defeasance or yield maintenance. | Defeasance or yield maintenance. |
| Tax & Insurance Escrows | Monthly deposits required. *May be waived if certain criteria are met.* | Monthly deposits required. |
| Replacement Reserves | Underwritten at a minimum of $(000) per unit per annum. *Monthly deposits may be waived if certain criteria are met.* | Underwritten at a minimum of $225 -$350 per unit per annum. |
| Origination Fee | From par to 3%. *This is in addition to closing costs.* | From par to 3%. *This is in addition to closing costs.* |
| Closing Cost | Deposit required for third party reports, processing costs, title and legal. | |
| Recourse | Case by case. In some cases non-recourse with standard exceptions for fraud and misrepresentations. Full non-recourse under 50% LTV. | Recourse and Non-Recourse Options |
| Subordinate Financing | Mezzanine allowed subject to approval. | |
| Assumable | Subject to approval and fee. | |
| **PROPERTY** | | |
| LTV / CLTV | Up to 75% | Up to 75% |
| DSCR | Minimum 1.25 | Minimum 1.30 |

| | | |
|---|---|---|
| Commercial Space | Maximum 20% of net rentable area and maxium 20% of effective gross income. | |
| Required Reports (ordered by Lender). | Narrative MAI Appraisal, Property Conditions Assessment, and Phase I. Others if applicable. | |

## 5.2   Lender Programs

| LENDER PROGRAMS | | |
|---|---|---|
| **Underwriting Profile** | **Program Highlights** | **Loan Purpose** |
| Stated:  Stated income & assets of borrower. Borrower must have 10% minimum equity.  Stated debt service coverage ratio.  Par & par plus pricing.  Fixed & adjustable rates. | Focuses on Borrower's credit score (middle score on tri-merge), personal financial strength, and actual rent roll. Appraisal must confirm all statements and property value.  Loan amount is usually up to $2,000,000.00 for qualified borrowers. | Purchase, Refinance, Cash-out Refinance. |
| Bridge:  Single asset special purpose entity with good overall credit with sufficient liquidity & demonstrated experience completing similar transactions.  Minimum DSC 1.10 "As-Is" & 1.25 at exit.  Maximum 90% LTV "As-Is" & 80% LTV at exit.  Monthly deposits required for tax and escrows.  Narrative MAI Appraisal, Property Condition Assessment and Phase I Environmental. First mortgage lien on subject property. | Rehab repositioning, quick acquisition, turnarounds, equity cash-out and creative financing.  Loan amount is usually from $2,000,000.00 up for qualified borrowers. | Allows time to reposition a property before obtaining permanent financing. Once the property is stabilized the Lender can offer a no hassle permanent loan. |

| Portfolio | A to C average & above properties (minor deferred maintenance considered). *Mixed use considered with no more than 25% of income derived from other than residential use.* |
|-----------|---------|
| Balloon | A to C average & above properties (minor deferred maintenance considered). *Mixed use considered with no more than 25% of income derived from other than residential use.* |

## 5.3    Loan Documentation

For the Broker/Bank to begin processing a loan, the following is required:

A.    Business Plan (for start-up or turnaround situations).
B.    Borrower's Information.
    a.    Financials (last 3 years of taxes, and W-2s).
C.    Business Information.
    a.    Date Business was started.
    b.    Form of Ownership.
        i    LLC Documents, Articles of Incorporation, Corporate Resolution.
    c.    Date of current ownership.
        i    Documentation on company ownership, including percent of ownership.
    d.    Business address and date business was moved to it.
    e.    Number of employees.
    f.    Resume of all members.
    g.    Financials (last 3 years of taxes).
    h.    List of outstanding obligations, loan balances, and monthly payment.
        i    Certified Profit and Loss Statement.
        ii    Other assets, and liabilities.
    i    A signed and dated financial statement on all members.
        i    Life Insurance held.
D.    Lender's Application.
E.    Property Information.
    a.    Certified Property Operating Statement.
    b.    Property Rent Roll.
    c.    Digital Color photographs of the Property.
    d.    See Appendix
F.    Copy of the executed Purchase and Sales Agreement (PSA).
G.    Additional information as required.

## Construction Loans

In addition to the above, construction loans require the following:

A. Pro forma statements based on completion of project, including cash-flow projections.
B. Property description, location, and cost information.
C. Loan request:
    a. Amount
    b. Term
    c. Repayment schedule
    d. Prepayment
    e. Tax and Insurance deposits
    f. Disbursement procedure (progress payments or voucher).
    g. Lien information.
D. Contractor Information.
    a. Names of general contractor and subcontractors.
        i Analysis of reputation of General Contractor and Sub-Contractors (Dun & Bradstreet reports).
    b. Actual cost calculations.
    c. Copy of plans and specifications.
    d. Copy of construction contract.
        i Bonding information (furnished by corporate surety acceptable to lenders, naming contractor, as principal, borrower as oblige, and lender as dual oblige. Penalty is full contract amount).
    e. Bond types:
        i Completion (guarantees improvement will be completed by a certain time).
        ii Performance (promises to stand behind agreement).
        iii Payment (guarantees all material men's and subcontractor's payment and clear of lien).
    f. Time line
E. Loan Analysis.
F. Borrower
    a. Management experience.
    b. Ratio of project cash flow to debt servicing requirements.
    c. Analysis of project effect on working capital in regard to other commitments.
    d. Need for personal guarantees (usually required unless construction loan agreement covenants provide substitutes, or unless past experience makes it unnecessary).
G. Property and Improvements
    a. Appraisal of market value of land.
    b. Review of existing encumbrances on the land.

## 5.4    Prequalification

If the deal is workable, a prequalification letter is issued to the Borrower.  This is a conditional approval, not a commitment, and all of the conditions and stipulations of the loan will be spelled out.  This Letter of Interest (LOI) will include the following information as it pertains to the loan:

- anticipated loan amount

- interest rate, points, fees

- rate lock policy

- up-front costs, and impounds

- third party reports

- assumption provisions

    o   closing time

    o   life time cap (if applicable); adjustment period and margin after fixed rate period is over

    o   floor pre-payment penalty

When you sign the LOI and make payment in full for the appraisal, the lender will order the appraisal.  The appraisal can take anywhere from 2-6 weeks.

**Note:  Never confuse "Prequalification" with "Preapproval."  Prequalification means that your numbers add-up, and generally speaking the Lender should (cursory) approve you.  Preapproval means that your paperwork has been submitted to the Lender and they have preapproved you for the loan subject to an appraisal of the property to be purchased.**

## 5.5    Borrower Submission Package

The Broker/Bank will prepare a submission package with all the documents that you have given to them, and what they have ordered.  This package is then sent to the Lender for their review.

## 5.6    Lenders Interview

Upon receipt of the loan submission package, the Lender's Underwriter verifies the completeness of the package and determines if it represents a viable loan.  During this process, some underwriters will conduct an in-depth telephone interview with the

Borrower to verify information provided, to obtain missing or unclear information and to get a better understanding of your business and its' operation.

Scoring:  The following shows a system in which applicants are scored.

a. <u>5 Points</u>

Management:  3 years of experience direct management in Apartment Buildings.

Repayment Ability:  DSC of 1.5:1 or better for 2 years plus interim, with positive or stable trends.

Collateral:  75 % LTV (based on property only.

Credit:  Clean credit, no present or past derogatory items, and "Beacon Score" of 760 or more.

Net Worth:  D/W of 2:1 or less.

Equity Injection:  At least 30% injection** with proforma D/W of 2:1 or less.

b. <u>4 Points</u>

Management:  At least 1-year direct management experience or 3 years of small business ownership experience.

Repayment Ability:  DSC of 1.25:1 or better for 2 years plus interim, or last FYE plus interim of 1.5:1.

Collateral:  80 % LTV (based on property only.

Credit:  Clean credit, no present or past derogatory items, and "Beacon Score" of less than 760.

Net Worth:  D/W of 3:1 or less.

Equity Injection:  At least 20% injection** with proforma D/W of 3:1 or less.

c. <u>3 Points</u>

Management:  Minimum of 2 years' industry experience (non-mgmt.) or 1 year of small business ownership experience.

Repayment Ability:  DSC of 1.15:1 or better in last FYE plus interim.

Collateral:  At least 50% R/E discounted collateral coverage with 100% total discounted collateral coverage *

Credit:  Minor delinquencies (not more than 3/30 day delinquencies within the past 24-month period, no 60+).

Net Worth:  D/W of 4:1 or less

Equity Injection:  At least 10% injection** with proforma D/W of 4:1 or less or 100% financing with a proforma D/W of less than 2:1.

d. 2 Points

Management:  Minimum of 1-year Apartment Building experience or management experience.

Repayment Ability:  DSC of 1.0:1 in last FYE or interim only (6 mo. Min.).

Collateral:  At least 67% total collateral coverage. *

Credit:  Serious delinquencies (30, 60, 90 day).

Net Worth:  D/W > 4:1 but less than 6:1

Equity injection:  10% financing with proforma D/W of 4:1 or less.

e. 1 Points

Management:  No experience

Repayment Ability:  Projections deal - no historical cash flow, or start-up.

Collateral:  Less than 67% collateral coverage*

Credit:  Collections, charge-offs, tax liens, or bankruptcy with acceptable explanation.

Net Worth:  D/W greater than 6:1.

Equity Injection:  100% financing with proforma D/W over 4:1.

f. Bonus Points

2 bonus points for outside income sufficient to service 50% + % of the proposed debt.

1 bonus point for outside income sufficient to service 25% + % of the proposed debt.

g. Ratings

| Excellent | 21-25 | * | Business assets at liquidation value. |
|-----------|-------|---|----------------------------------------|
| Good | 17-20 | | |
| Fair | 15-16 | ** | Cash or real estate equity. |
| Marginal | 13-14 | | |
| Decline | 12 or less | *** Use either but not both. | |

## 5.7    Commitment Letter

With a favorable report, the application package is sent to the Lender's Underwriting Committee for approval.  Once approved, a Commitment Letter will be sent to you for review and approval.  Upon your acceptance of the commitment letter, the Lender will order Title, and all other necessary reports to process and underwrite the loan.

## 5.8    Personal Assessment

Before going to a Mortgage Broker or Bank to obtain a loan for investment property, you might consider undertaking a personal assessment of your financial situation.

## SECTION 6    MULTIFAMILY HOUSES

### 6.0    Definition

A **Commercial Multifamily** is any building or group of buildings that contain five or more units. For the purpose of this book, we will refer to Multifamily Houses as those that contain from five (5) to eleven (11) dwelling units. These units can be in the form of a single low-rise building, two-story garden style building, or townhouses.

**Fannie Mae and Freddie Mac** establish guidelines for residential loans, and how they are resold in the secondary market. Properties with five or more units are commercial properties according to the guidelines, and are not eligible for *residential funding*.

### 6.1    Purchasing Guidelines

Purchase multifamily housing containing 5 to 11 units. An ideal building will have a good mix of one, two, and three-bedroom apartments. Buildings with all studios or one-bedroom units tend to stay empty longer (unless you are next to a college or university) since they significantly limit your tenant base. Always refer to the complex as a "community" rather than its legal (ABC LLC) name in non-legal matters. The communities should be well located (they command better sales prices and higher rents), that is near public transportation, shopping, and other attractions.

Multifamily Houses require commercial loans of which there are two types:

- Small Balance Commercial Loans: Conventional Bank (depending on loan size).

- Regular Commercial Loan: Commercial Bank or Specialty Lender.

*Note: If you put 20% down, and the computations provide a negative cash flow, you should avoid purchasing the property especially if there is no significant upside or value-add play in sight.*

### 6.2    Rent Increases

There are two types of rent increases:

- Economic increase: This is a large increase in the monthly rent due to factors of which you have no control such as tax increases, higher utility bills, and of course inflation.

- Nuisance raise: This small increase (5 to 10 percent) gives you an increase in rentable income and does not force the tenant to leave and find another apartment, incur the cost of moving, changing addresses, telephone numbers etc. The tenant just stays and pays the small increase.

## 6.3  Management

Because of the size and number of rental units, Multifamily Housing is ideal for an onsite superintendent or Resident Manager, as I prefer to call them.  This Resident Manager has a lot of responsibilities, and also presents some liabilities to you.

## 6.4  Using Investment Measurements

Illustration:  Purchase multifamily w/6 units + billboard for $260,000.  Mortgage $200,000 @5% for 15 years.  P&I = $18,979.04 year.

| Operating Revenues | AMOUNT | % |
|---|---|---|
| Potential Rental Income | $48,000 | 96.97 |
| Other Income | 1,500 | 3.03 |
| Less:  Vacancy & Credit Losses | (2,400) | 4.85 |
| **Gross Operating Income (GOI)** | **$47,100** | **95.15** |
| Operating Expenses | | |
| Insurance | $2,900 | 30.48 |
| Property Taxes | 3,773 | 39.65 |
| Trash Removal | 1,500 | 15.76 |
| Water | 980 | 10.30 |
| Miscellaneous | 362 | 3.80 |
| **Total Operating Expense** | **$9,515** | **100.00** |
| **Net Operating Income (NOI)** | **$37,585** | 75.93 |
| **Debt Service** | (18,979) | 38.34 |
| **Net Cash Flow** | **$18,606** | **37.59** |

# SECTION 7 APARTMENT BUILDINGS / COMPLEXES

## 7.0 Apartment Buildings

An **Apartment Building** is any building or group of buildings that contain twelve or more units. As a prudent investor, we recommend that you invest in properties fewer than 125 units. These units can be in the form of a single low-rise building, a single mid-rise building, a single high-rise building, two-story garden style buildings, or townhouses.

Purchasing larger complexes (over 150 units) will put you in direct competition with institutional buyers and their deep pockets.

## 7.1 Building Classifications

Apartment buildings are classified as A, B, C, and D. Generally speaking, the difference is cost per unit, age of building, improvements and amenities.

## 7.2 Purchasing Guidelines

Purchase Apartment Buildings containing 12 to 125 units. An ideal building will have a good mix of one, two, and three-bedroom apartments. Always refer to the complex as a "Community" rather than its legal (ABC LLC) name in non-legal matters. The communities should be well located (they command better sales prices and higher rents), near public transportation, shopping, and other attractions.

Apartment Buildings/Complexes require commercial loans of which there are two types:

- Small Balance Commercial Loans: Conventional Bank (depending on loan size).

- Regular Commercial Loan: Commercial Bank or Specialty Lender.

*Note: If you put 20% down, and the computations provide a negative cash flow, you should avoid purchasing the property especially if there is no significant upside or value-add play in sight.*

## 7.3 Rent Increases

There are three types of rental increases:

- Economic increase: This is a large increase in the monthly rent (12% to 15%) due to factors of which you have no control such as tax increases, higher utility bills, and of course inflation.

- Regulatory: This increase is regulated by a government authority, and you have no control over the amount or when it occurs.

- Nuisance raise: This small increase (5 to 10 percent) gives you an increase in rentable income and does not force the tenant to leave and find another apartment, incur the cost of moving, changing addresses, telephone numbers etc. The tenant just stays and pays the small increase.

## 7.4 Management

According to the size or how you wish to **run** your property, there are two options, the Resident Manager (RM) or a Professional Management Company (PMC). Both management types have their unique advantages and disadvantages. If your investment properties do not have many units, I would recommend having the Resident Manager (it gives you more control and different tax benefits). If the acquisition is large, then the obvious choice is the PMC.

## 7.5 Professional Management Company (PMC)

Aside from the obvious reason for hiring a Professional Management Company, the non-obvious is liability. Through the hiring of a PMC, the liability for a multitude of problems becomes their problems. Major benefits are

- the PMC is an independent entity and not an employee

- your LLC is in the background and not subject to scrutiny from the public

- the PMC is liable for Federal, State, and local laws

- the PMC is responsible for employment personnel (harassment and discrimination laws, dispute resolution)

- tenant law

- gives you more time to expand your portfolio

**Before Selecting**

- obtain a copy of the property management agreement for review by both you and your attorney

- obtain company references

- address of similar properties under their management

  o drive-by and research their on-site staff

- caution

o When using small management, companies confirm that they have enough resources to operate efficiently. *Small may be better than none!* Especially from a liability view

## When Selecting a Professional Property Management Company

Obtain a written service agreement, signed and dated by you and the management company. The agreement should state in bold letters that the Management Company is an **independent contractor** and not an employee. This document will serve as a roadmap and guide describing the obligations of both parties. Typically, the agreement should outline the following key elements:

A. Identification of all parties and the property.

B. Contract period: Usually no longer than one year. Review the termination causes. You want the ability to terminate the agreement prior to the termination date for cause (30-day cancellation clause is normal).

C. Authority and responsibilities of the management company: This section should detail what you expect to get in return for the management fee

   a. onsite staffing (hiring, supervising, terminating

   b. supervision by the management agent and staff

   c. general maintenance of books and records including general ledger, accounts payable, payroll, accounts receivable, etc.

   d. preparation and distribution of payroll for all onsite employees including appropriate tax reports, unemployment, and Worker's Compensation reports

   e. management agent overhead, including

   - travel of agent staff to property for onsite inspections, training, or supervision

   - insurance coverage for agent's office and operations (property, auto, liability, errors and omissions, workers' compensation, etc.)

   - telephone expense

   - postage expense related to normal responsibility for mailing to the property

   - establishment, maintenance and control of an accounting system adequate to carry out accounting supervision responsibilities

- maintenance of bank accounts and monthly reconciliations

- development, preparation, and revision of management plan or agreements

- account maintenance, settlement and disbursement of security deposits

- storage of records

- oversight of general and preventive maintenance procedures and policies

- full disclosure if the Maintenance Company has a relationship with the Management Company

**Note: The management fee is always negotiable and should consist of a percent of the gross collected income produced on a month-to-month basis, and retention of current residents.**

f.  Minimum Required Reports

- monthly **Rent Roll** detailing each individual unit, who the occupant is, what type of unit they're renting, the current rental rate, security deposit, the day it was rented and the date the lease expires, any delinquent rent owed, and any other income the resident is responsible for paying

- monthly **Disbursement Report and Receipts**. Chronological list of every bill paid, including the invoice. List of outstanding bills. *The pricing on repairs must be verified to be competitive since many Management Companies have sister companies that handle the maintenance*

- weekly **Vacancy and Delinquency Report** via FAX. This report should contain the condition of each vacant unit, when it was vacated, and if there are any new residents scheduled to move-in

- **Operating Statement** detailing all income and expenses both monthly and year to date. It should also measure current operations against the budget

- investor responsibilities: Some generally accepted items that may be paid out of the operating account are

  o  actual costs for full-time and part-time staff, including managers, maintenance staff and temporary help

  o  gross salary

  o  employer Federal Insurance Contribution Act (FICA) tax

- State and Federal Unemployment tax

- Workers' Compensation Insurance

- health insurance premiums

- performance incentives

- traveling expenses (for business or training)

g. All repair and maintenance costs relating to the operation of the property.

- maintenance staff

- supplies

- turnover maintenance (paint, flooring, appliances, etc.)

- preventive maintenance

- other maintenance (elevator, pest control, landscaping, etc.)

- contract repairs (roofing, exterior paint, etc.)

h. Other Expenses

- credit and background checks related to prospective residents

- bank charges (checks, service fees, NSF check fees, deposit slips)

- advertising

- telephone expense

- utility expense

- property insurance

- repairs and maintenance

- real estate taxes (personal and property)

- insurance (property liability and casualty)

- management fee

- Compensation Structure: The management agreement should contain a clause specifying the compensation structure for managing the property

| CLASSIFICATION OF APARTMENT BUILDINGS | | | |
|---|---|---|---|
| CLASS | DESCRIPTION | PRO'S | CON'S |
| A | Usually $75,000 and up per unit. Less than 10 years old. Commands the highest price per unit due to new(er) construct-ion, building materials, and labor costs | Higher rents and lower maintenance costs. These buildings usually have amenities such as swimming pools and weight rooms. | Highest price per-unit on resale, and lowest initial rate of return. In a down economy, these are the first to empty and/or have delinquen-cies. These units offer the least upside potential since there is no additional value to create. |
| B | Priced from $25,000 to $75,000 per unit. The buildings range between 10 and 20 years old and are in relatively good condition. These properties are often located in solid middle-income areas and **are likely the most stable** among the various property classes. | Most of the building deterior-ation is aesthetic and can be easily repaired. The mechanical and electrical systems are near ready for repair or overhaul. | These buildings represent good value and are prime for creating real value. |
| C | Priced from $10,000 to $30,000 per unit. The buildings range between 20 to 30 years old and, are in good condition. These properties are often located in stable neighborhoods and have not suffered from deteriorating conditions in the surrounding area. | Cosmetic improvements can do wonders as can the addition of some amenities that the Class A & B building have. If you can find a Class C in a Class B neighborhood, you have a real winner. Modernizing the individual units with updated appliances and cabinets is an affordable way to add value. Most of these buildings can be sub-metered. The mechanical and electrical systems are ready or near ready for repair or overhaul. | Selection of Class C apartments must be made carefully due to the influx of high crime in the surrounding area |
| D | Priced from $5,000 to $10,000 per unit. The buildings are generally in excess of 30 years in age. | These building are naturals for value-add features as long as capital funds are available. Typical repairs or replace-ments are roofs, parking lot surfaces, heating and cooling equipment, and boiler equipment. Usually at this age the complete electrical system must be replaced. | Selection of Class C apartments must be made carefully due to the influx of high crime in the surrounding area |

# SECTION 8  PROFILE OF A MULTIFAMILY INVESTOR

## 8.0  Your Income

Before you can make a financial investment, you must have the capital or income to do so. According to the Internal Revenue Code, there are three categories of income:

**Ordinary Income:** That which is earned through the performance of a personal service. You *earn* a salary for the performance of a personal service to another (your boss). Ordinary income earned by wages, corporation income, estates income and trust income is subject to Federal Taxation. Additionally, salaries are subject to FICA (Social Security and Medicare) taxes, which take an additional 7.65 percent of an employee's salary and 15.3 percent of a self-employed individual's income. Ordinary income also includes interest and certain types of dividends but these two income sources are not subject to FICA.

- Most states impose a tax on federal taxable income of individuals, corporations, estates, and trusts. Alaska, Florida, Nevada, South Dakota, Texas, Washington, and Wyoming have no state income tax. Additionally, New Hampshire and Tennessee limit their state income tax to only dividends and interest income.

**Tax-free income:** This is income that does not increase wealth, or is labeled tax free due to tax code such as tax-free municipal and state bonds.

**Capital Gain:** This is the most important type of income for real estate investors, since it is the result of the sale or exchange of rental property. Capital gains are either short term (held for less than one year) or long term (held for one year and a day or more).

There are additional taxes which the government subjects us too, such as State Sales Tax; Fuel Tax, Cigarette Tax; Personal Income Tax; Retirement Income Tax; Property Tax; Property Tax by County; Inheritance and Estate Taxes; tax for working in an adjacent state and just too much more that is beyond the scope of this book.

## 8.1  Assumptions

To continue, let us assume that you have the initial investment (you can also use your 401K, or savings) to make your purchase. You are married, and both you and your spouse are W2 workers. You have seen all the infomercials, heard the horror stories, and somehow you were directed to this book, and now you are ready to make the leap to becoming a *real estate investor specializing in multifamily housing.* (GREAT CHOICE!)

**Note: During the early stages of your new career you will most likely be an active investor, then gradually progressing to a real estate professional.**

## 8.2    The Steps

A.   Prepare and write your Business Plan

B.   Decide on your farm location[6] and complete

- research

- your Property Research Table

- all farming documentation

- TOWS Chart

C.   Select your professional group of advisors

D.   Select your trade team members

D.   Open your "Purchase" Money Market Account

E.   Select your first property

F.   Make your OFFER

- consult your attorney

- contract signing / due diligence

- lender

- form your llc

- obtain insurance quotes

G.   Ownership

- open a "Trust" Money Market Account in LLC name

- open "Disbursement" LLC account


## 8.3    Investor Qualifications

An investor holds real property primarily for appreciation.  Only investors can qualify for like-kind exchanges or installment sales tax treatment.  The IRS categorizes rental income as passive income, even if you materially participate in rental activity, unless you are a *real estate professional*.

Again, rental real estate is considered a passive activity, and loses from passive activities may only be used to offset income from passive activities.  There are two rules that limit the amount of loss that you can deduct from an income producing property:

---

[6] Use (ISBN 13:978 1540896858) How to Start and Propagate Your Farm as a guide.

A. At risk (applies to property put into use after 1986) is the investment that you would lose, or the capital that you have at risk. When calculating the amount of capital at risk, the following amounts can be included

- cash contributed to the investment activity

- the adjusted tax basis of other property contributed to the activity

- money that was borrowed for which you are personally liable, or other property used as collateral

- borrowed money for which you are not personally liable provided the nonrecourse loans meet certain conditions

B. Your passive activity limits are based on the amount of capital that you have at risk, unless you are a *real estate professional.*

If you qualify as a *real estate professional*, you can use rental property tax losses to offset taxable income from other sources. An unlimited amount of loss deductions as an adjustment to the Adjusted Gross Income (AGI) can be made. To qualify you must pass two tests

- more than half of all personal services performed during the year must be qualified real estate activities in which you materially participated

- you must perform at least 750 hours of service per year in those real estate activities

C. What qualifies as real estate activities?

- development; rent related activities; operating activities; acquisition activities; and management.

Carrying Forward Unused Losses (Suspended Losses): If you have passive loses, and do not qualify for either the active participation exception or the real estate professional exception, you can carry your passive losses forward to future (indefinite) years. In most cases, the losses will be carried forward and taken in the year the property is sold.

A. Taxable Write-offs: If you are qualified as an active investor (you make major decisions, determine rental rates, capital improvements, major repairs, new resident standards, etc.) the IRS offers a $25,000 write-off against salaries and other non-passive income. The following conditions apply

- the property must be rental real estate

- you must be an individual taxpayer. The deduction is not available to a corporation or limited partner

- if you make an annual gross income of $125,000.00 per year or more, the maximum deduction of $25,000.00 is reduced. If you earn $150,000.00 or more, you are exempt

- you must be at least a 10% owner of the property

## 8.4 Forms of Property

There are three basic forms of property related to real estate: real property, personal property, and fixtures. Separating the value of real property and fixtures is necessary for calculating depreciation deductions.

- real property is divided into two entities: land and its improvements

- fixtures are permanently attached to real property

- personal property is an asset that is moveable and not attached to the property

## 8.5 Taxable Strategies

The following strategies are intended to be a guide for the accumulation of wealth through a variety of real estate investments that depend on the careful and effective use of *existing tax codes* to accelerate the growth of wealth and preserve wealth once acquired.

Just as important, this book includes information on how to develop a plan effectively using tax code at different times in your investment career to maximize the effect. I.e. The early part of your career should focus on acquiring property and gaining a foothold. Later, you have several choices; maximizing the income derived from the property, or owning multiple properties providing multiple streams of income, or focusing wealth in only a few high value properties.

Pursuing one of these strategies without paying capital gain and other taxes should be part of your overall plan. Once wealth is obtained, it is time to create dependable, tax-minimized income streams to provide a reliable retirement income. Properly done, a well-planned wealth accumulation strategy delivers amazing results through compounding interest and the use of other people's money to invest in the most dependable appreciating asset.

## R E A L   E S T A T E!

Capital Gains

Since your *business is real estate investment*, all of your properties when sold are long-term capital gains. Capital Gains are taxed at the rate of 15% which must be paid on all properties sold, unless deferred through a **1031 exchange**.

The following is an example of **Short Term, and Long Term Capital Gain**. As illustrated, the difference of $32,500.00 is realized by just holding on to the asset for twelve plus months.

- Simple Illustration

|  | Short-Term Capital Gain | Long-Term Capital Gains |
|---|---|---|
| **Purchase Price:** | $1,000,000.00 | $1,000,000.00 |
| **Sales Price:** | $1,250,000.00 | $1,250,000.00 |
| **Capital Gain:** | $250,000.00 | $250,000.00 |
| **Tax Rate:** | 33% | 20% |
| **Taxes Due:** | $82,500.00 | $50,000.00 |
| **Difference = $82,500.00 - $50,000.00 = $32,500.00** | | |

## 8.6 Alternative Minimum Tax (AMT)

The AMT is an extra tax that may have to be paid on top of regular income tax. Designed by the IRS so that high-income taxpayers would not be able to pay little or no taxes by using deductions and exclusions. Overtime the AMT has expanded, and it now impacts many taxpayers who do not have high income.

The AMT provides an alternative method for calculating your income tax. If this calculation produces a higher tax liability than the regular calculation, then the taxpayer must pay the higher amount.

## 8.7 Tax Deductions

The following is a short list of tax deductions (expenses) that you can subtract from the amount of income tax you pay. Consult with your accountant for additional benefits!

| DEDUCTIONS | DEFINITION |
|---|---|
| Cleaning and Maintenance | Salaries of employees or contractors hired to clean and maintain properties and/or materials purchased for cleaning and maintaining. |
| Management Fees | Money paid to a Resident Manager or Property Management Company. |
| Professional Fees | Fees paid to the tax accountant, bookkeeper, attorney, and other professionals hired to help service your investment. |
| Pest Control | Cost of exterminator services. |
| Supplies | Price of tools used to maintain rental property, landscaping supplies, cleaning supplies, etc. |
| Equipment | Machinery purchased for your rental property, including lawn mowers, snow blowers, etc. |
| Repairs | Bills for outside contractors hired to make repairs. |
| Advertising | Costs of advertising your rental property (fees for classified ads, materials for signs). |
| Utilities | If you pay for utilities such as electricity and/or gas and water, you can deduct these operating expenses. |
| Professional association dues and educational materials | Cost of membership for any property owners' associations you belong to; cost of books, magazine subscriptions, classes, and other education on land lording. |
| Insurance Premiums | Premiums paid for any insurance on your rental property. |
| Mortgage Interest | Annual interest paid for mortgages on rental properties. |
| Property Taxes | Any property taxes you pay on rental properties. |
| Home Office Expenses | Costs of having a home office; current auto mileage (54.0 cents) on business travel. |

## 8.8   Property Depreciation

For rental property, there are three methods that can be used to calculate depreciation depending on the type of property and when you placed it in service.  The only one that will apply to you is MACRS.

- MACRS (Modified Accelerated Cost Recovery System) for property placed in service after 1986.

- ACRS (Accelerated Cost Recovery System) for property placed in service after 1980 but before 1987.

- Useful lives and either straight line or an accelerated method of depreciation, for property placed in service before 1981.

## 8.9   Depreciable Basis

The Cost Basis is the amount paid for the property

Amount Paid + Settlement Cost + Closing Costs = Cost Basis

Settlement Cost include legal recording fees; abstract fees; survey charges; owners title insurance; amounts the seller owes that you agree to pay, such as back taxes, or interest, recording or mortgage fees, charges for improvements or repairs, and sales commissions.

**Note:  Improvements made after the property was placed into service must be accounted for separately.**

## 8.10   Recaptured Depreciation, and Capital Gains Taxes

Depreciation works well to shield income (earnings) from rental properties, although it has a negative tax consequence when the time comes to sell the property.

- Formula:  Original Investment + Capitalized Improvements - Depreciation = Adjusted Basis + Purchase Expenses

When rental properties are sold for more than the adjusted basis, a capital gain occurs. The depreciation taken over the years assumed the property was being *"used-up"* in the course of business.  The increased value at the time of sale (*capital gain*) triggers the need to recover depreciation because the value of the property did not decrease.  The 25 percent depreciation recapture tax is applied to the smaller of these two amounts:

- total depreciation allowed on the property (whether the depreciation was taken or not)

- the total gain from the property sale if it is less than the depreciation taken

## 8.11   Installment Sales for Tax Deferral

Real estate investors can defer payment of capital gains taxes and depreciation recapture taxes by accepting installment sales.  This is not *the indefinite deferral of taxes* in the same way as a 1031 exchange.

Installment Sales are most appropriate when

- an income stream is desirable for retirement or other income.  This income is taxed at the lower long-term capital gain rate (to the extent that it represents profit).  A higher sales price and a lower interest rate can mean more profit taxed at the lower long-term capital gain rate

- the interest rate earned exceeds other investment opportunities

- the property is not producing income, and other income producing opportunities are more appealing

- enhances the marketability of the real estate justifying a higher selling price

- an exit strategy paying deferred taxes with inflated dollars is the best alternative

**Note: The IRS recaptures depreciation when you sell investment property for more than its basis if a 1031 deferred exchange is not used.**

## 8.12  Installment Sale Payments

Each payment received on an installment sale has three components:  interest income, return of adjusted basis, and profit or gain on the sale.

Taxes have to be paid in the tax year that the installment payments are received, including any down payment received at the time of sale.  These taxes are paid only on the gross profit.  To calculate what percentage of the total contract price from the deal is gross profit

- determine the total gross profit (is equal to the selling price minus the adjusted basis) for the sale

- determine the gross profit percentage (is equal to the selling price minus the adjusted basis) for the sale

- for each taxable year, determine the taxable gain by multiplying the gross profit percent by the actual payments received

If you are providing **Seller Financing** the following, **installment items** need to be addressed in the contractual terms

- adequate down payment for security, but low enough to minimize taxes due

- enough down payment so that net funds to you (seller) are enough to pay depreciation recapture taxes (25%) due

- the amount of interest charged **stated interest** must be high enough (but lower than a bank) so that the IRS does not re-characterize part of the principal amount of the loan as interest.  Interest income is taxed as ordinary income tax rates

**Note:  When providing "Seller Financing" have your attorney draft the installment contract. Then, have your tax advisor calculate the taxes on the installment sale.**

- a clause protecting you against the buyer paying the loan off early (that would trigger taxes) and you losing your tax deferral

- a clause allowing a qualified buyer to assume the mortgage, if the original buyer sells the property, you want an opportunity to avoid the entire loan being paid in full

## 8.13  Installment Sales in 1031 Exchange

Combining an *installment sale with a 1031 exchange* can be an effective way to accomplish important financial goals.  (I.e. The installment sale will create a dependable income stream, and the down payment can be used to exchange into a replacement property).  This is another method of reducing tax obligation while preserving wealth.

**Tax strategies are difficult to understand, are continuously changing, and require the expert advice of a legal or tax professional.  We have brought some of the strategies that are available to you in this section so that you can visualize and be aware of, and be able to discuss them with your legal or tax professional.**

# SECTION 9     1031 TAX DEFERRED EXCHANGES

## 9.0    1031 Tax Deferred Exchange

Section 1031 of the Internal Revenue Code (IRC) allows an investor to sell an investment property and defer federal and state capital gain taxes if they are exchanged (or traded) into another **like-kind** property (as defined by the IRS.)  Like-kind means an investment property such as:

- Apartment Buildings

- Commercial Properties

- Single Family Residence (SFR) as a rental

- Duplex

- Raw land

**There is no limit on the number of times you can complete a 1031 exchange. Yes, it is possible to indefinitely defer taxes by continually exchanging properties.**

## 9.1    Common Terminology for 1031 Tax Deferment Properties are:

- the property being sold is referred to as the **down-leg** or **relinquished property**

- the property being purchased is referred to as the **up-leg** or **replacement property**

- using a 1031 exchange to purchase a more expensive property is called **trading up**

- using a 1031 exchange to purchase a property of less value than the relinquished property is called **trading down**

- **boot** - a term used to describe any taxable money or other benefit in an exchange that you elect to take

- **debit-reduction boot** occurs when the debt on the replacement property is less than the debt owned on the relinquished property

- **nonqualified expense boot** is using sales proceeds to pay for costs other than qualified closing expenses

- **excessive borrowing** more money than necessary to close on replacement property will likely result in boot

**Note: Capital Gains must be paid on the boot in the year in which it is taken.**

## 9.2    There Are Three Types of Exchanges:

Simultaneous Exchanges, where the relinquished property is transferred at the same time as the replacement property is received.  With the exception of a direct trade between two property holders, a third part is needed in the transaction to facilitate the acquisition or sale of one of the properties and then to complete the exchange.

**Delayed**, **Deferred**, or **Starker Exchanges**, where the relinquished property is transferred prior to the time the replacement property is received.  This requires the use of a third party to sell and buy the properties involved, and to hold the proceeds from the sale of the relinquished property.

**Reverse Exchanges**, where the replacement property is acquired by a third party for the exchanger prior to the time a sale has been arranged for the relinquished property.  At some point in the transaction, the replacement property is simultaneously exchanged for the relinquished property that is then sold.

## 9.3    Accommodators

These professional intermediaries are normally attorneys certified in Taxation Law, Estate Planning, Trust and Probate Law by their State Bar.  Before using one, verify that they are bonded and insured against errors and omissions (E&O), and employee dishonesty.  Part of the services that they provide are to

- confer with potential Exchangers and their tax and legal advisers regarding availability and the structure of an exchange

- prepare the Exchange Agreement, escrow instructions, and related documents

- confer with the title or escrow company to facilitate the exchange

- hold and invest any funds that must be held as part of the transaction.  Interest earned on the funds is paid to the Exchanger after the transaction is completed

- prepare tax reporting documents for the interest earned on held funds

## 9.4    Reasons for using the 1031 Deferred Exchange:

- Exchange to defer capital gains tax

- Exchange from a fully depreciated property to a higher value property that can be fully depreciated

- Exchange from a larger property to several smaller properties to divide an estate among children or for retirement reasons

- Exchange for a property that may be easier to sell in the future

- Exchange from a slowly appreciating property to a property in an area with faster appreciation

- Exchange from a partial interest in one property to a full interest in another

- Exchange from several smaller properties, to one large property to consolidate the benefits of ownership, and reduce management responsibilities

- Exchange from a property with maximized or minimal cash flow to a property with larger cash flow

- Exchange to fit the life style desired whereas a retiree may want reduced management for travel opportunities

- Exchange to meet local requirements

- Exchange to reposition assets

- Exchange from one property type to another property type

- Exchange to increase leverage

## 9.5   Timeline

The IRS allows up to a maximum of 180 calendar days *(the exchange period)* between the sale of your down-leg and the purchase of your up-leg property.  When your relinquished property sells, you have 45 calendar days from closing to identify in writing a suitable replacement property.

The 1031 Deferred Exchange must close before the taxpayer's next date to file a tax return with the IRS.  Filing extensions are allowed so the full 180 days can run-out.

## 9.6   The "Three Property Rule"

Most real estate investors provide three different properties that they are interested in buying as their replacement property.

## 9.7   The 200% Rule

This rule allows the identification of an unlimited number of properties as long as the total of all prices is not more than twice the price of the property being sold.

The 200% rule works well when making an exchange for multiple properties.

## 9.8   Effect of a 1031 Deferred Exchange on Depreciable Value

The adjusted depreciation carries forward from the relinquished property to the replacement property.  The result being that only the depreciation that remained from the relinquished property, plus any additional capital (loans or the owner's money), are available for the depreciation write-off on the replacement property.

# SECTION 10    WEALTH, GOALS AND STRATEGIES

## 10.0  Wealth

Generally speaking, your wealth is everything that you own minus everything that you owe. Not planning your wealth can become a headache for your beneficiaries. Your beneficiaries include your spouse, children, grandchildren, and charitable organizations.

Another word for wealth is estate. A well-designed estate plan incorporates a will, trusts, power of attorney, and other financial entities. The primary purpose of creating an estate is to arrange your affairs in a fashion so that the entire estate is passed on as you direct.

A. A will is a basic form of expressing your wishes and how you want them carried out. A will should always be prepared in conjunction with an attorney. Once prepared, both you and your attorney should have a signed (*executed*) copy. Probate is the process in which a will is validated and its directives are carried out. (The Probate process is an expensive process for the estate).

B. A better option to creating a will is called a trust. A trust not only answers who gets what, but it spells out when and how. Avoiding probate is the main reason that the wealthiest people choose this form of protection. Remember, in order to work properly the trust should be prepared by an attorney.

C. A revocable living trust creates a holding form of ownership for assets during a person's lifetime, and for distribution of the assets after death. A major benefit of this trust is that your heirs will not have to go through probate. The trustee will deliver assets to the named beneficiaries without any court involvement. A living trust also minimizes estate taxes.

D. For 2017 the lifetime gift and tax exclusion is $5,490,000 per person, while the maximum estate and gift tax rate remains 40%. Current law permits portability (the transfer of any unused federal tax exclusion to a surviving spouse). Using the unlimited marital deduction to transfer all assets to the surviving spouse and using the Deceased Spousal Unused Exclusion (DSUE), your spouse may be able to inherit more than $10,980,00 of your assets without incurring federal estate taxes. Totally separate, the annual gift exclusion allows you to gift $14,000 each to a person, or $28,000 for a married couple, to as many individuals as you would like to without going into your lifetime exemption. Note these numbers change annually for inflation.

**Note:  Assets held in joint tenancy are not controlled by your will or trust. The only assets controlled by your will are those assets titled in your name**

**only and that do not have a beneficiary designation. Assets titled in a revocable trust can be administered without probate.**

## 10.1 Asset Protection

Asset Protection[7] has two goals, to minimize the risk of potential liability, and to preserve assets. To protect your personal assets from lawsuits and creditors there are several strategies to consider:

- If you are the incidental owner of your life insurance policy, (it could cost your heirs up to 55%).

- Never do business as a sole proprietor, but as a LLC.

- Never do business as a general partnership (you may be held responsible for your partner's liabilities).

- Separate all of your assets into different legal entities (i.e. do not own your personal residence in the same financial entity as your investment apartment buildings).

- Never make your worth known, it could trigger frivolous lawsuits.

- You cannot be sued for what you do not have.

- Buy adequate business insurance policies (they provide for your defense). In case of a major catastrophe, no matter how much you could afford on insurance it will never be enough. Liability insurance policies cover **actual losses**. They DO NOT cover **punitive damages**, **jury awards**, or other costs over and above actual damages.

- A good asset protection plan will

  o spread out your control over your assets

  o protect your current and future lifestyle

  o keep the ownership of your assets confidential and hard to find

  o discourage litigation and promote settlements in your favor

  o hedge against potential governmental, economic, and personal instability

---

[7] See (ISBN 13: 978 1540765246) Asset Protection for the Real Estate Investor and Other Professionals for information.

## 10.2  **Family Limited Liability Company** (FLLC)

The FLLC is a business entity that insulates its owners (called members) from the liabilities of the entity but is taxed for income purposes like a partnership.  The owners of the FLLC are family members.  The FLLC remains in existence until the earlier of unanimous consent of all members to dissolve, the expiration of a fixed term, or a judicial dissolution.

Managers manage and control the FLLC's business.  The managers decide when to make a distribution to members which, when made, must be proportionate to each member's interest in the FLLC.  The operating agreement may provide for one manager to control most FLLC activities including distributions to members.

The FLLC may own closely held businesses, real estate, marketable securities, or LLC's except for other entities that have elected to be taxed as "S" corporations.  The family's control of the FLLC assets will remain vested in the managers, but the members may gift during their lifetime or transfer at death their interests in the FLLC.

Advantages of the FLLC are

- preservation of a family's wealth in the family

- FLLC meetings may promote or facilitate family communication regarding wealth, investment philosophies and other family values

- control of FLLC assets will be vested in the managers.  The successor to a manager will also be determined by the operating agreement

- families with diversified investment portfolios are able to gift membership interests to younger generation family members without breaking up the diversified portfolio

- the FLLC should substantially reduce the estate or gift tax burden that is imposed on wealth that is transferred to family members because the FLLC should be valued as a growing concern, rather than at its liquidation value

- the FLLC protects member assets from the creditors of members.  A creditor of a member may only obtain a charging order against the member's interest in the FLLC and not its underlying assets

- members are insulated from liability for the FLLC's activities

- the FLLC may distribute cash or other assets proportionately to its members without triggering gain or loss

Federal Tax Attributes

- the FLLC is taxed as a partnership with each member reporting his or her own proportionate share of income or loss

- the FLLC must file partnership tax returns

## 10.3  Family Trusts

A trust exists when one person (a **trustee**) holds and owns property for the benefit of another person (a **beneficiary**).  A Family Trust is a trust set-up (usually Mom and Dad) to benefit **members of the family**.  The purpose of the Family Trust is to progressively transfer your assets to the trust, so that legally you own no assets yourself, but through the trust, you still have control over and receive the benefits of those assets.  The terms and conditions under which a family trust is established and maintained are set out in a **trust deed**.

The goal of a Family Trust is to transfer your significant assets from personal ownership to ownership by the trust or to achieve **personal poverty** while becoming a beneficiary of the trust yourself.  In doing this you succeed in protecting your assets from various threats such as claims by business creditors, or partners under the PROPERTY (RELATIONS) ACT 1976.

If you and your wife set-up a family trust you can delegate a trustee (or person with legal authority to act) on your behalf if you should both die at the same time.  This type of trust is called a **Discretionary Trust**.  This trustee will decide how much, and when income from the trust can be distributed to the beneficiaries.

Common features of these trust are

- a family member, for the benefit of other members of the family group establishes a trust

- the trustee may be subject to a family election, which provides them with certain tax advantages, provided that the trust passes the family control test and makes distributions of trust income only to the beneficiaries of the trust who are within the family group

- the family trust can assist in protecting the family group's assets from the liabilities of one or more of the family members (for instance, in the event of a family member's bankruptcy or insolvency)

- the family trust provides a mechanism to pass family assets to future generations

- the trust can provide a means of accessing favorable taxation treatment by ensuring all family members use their income tax Tax-free thresholds

- the trustee can distribute income that is distributed to the beneficiaries in any way they see fit, provided distributions are made to people who qualify as beneficiaries

    o  a trust may help avoid challenges of a will following the death of the settlor o   a trust may own a Limited Liability Company

Properly drafted and managed Family Trusts are a powerful tax planning tool. They also have other uses that are of equal if not greater importance such as

- Asset Protection – Assets transferred to a trust no longer belong to the grantor. The trust assets cannot be attached by the creditors of the grantor due to bankruptcy, dissolution of marriage, or a court award

- Tax planning – Inheritance tax would be eliminated because the trustee would not die upon the death of the grantor

- Avoiding probate expense and delays – Death has no effect on the trust assets which will continue to be held and managed in confidence by the trustees in accordance with the terms of the trust

- Confidentiality – Assets in a trust are completely confidential. Assets NOT in a trust goes to probate with or without a will

- Estate planning – Many people do not want their assets to pass outright to their heirs, whether chosen by them or as prescribed by law. A Family Trust is the most flexible way to accomplish their wants

- Protects the weak – Can provide for those who may be unable to manage their own affairs (such as children, the aged, disabled etc.)

- Preserving family assets – Can ensure that wealth accumulated over a lifetime is not divided-up amongst the heirs but retained as one fund to accumulate further, with distribution of payment to family members as the need arises while preserving some assets for future generations

- Continuing family business – Terms of the trusts will ensure that the wish for continuing the family business continues

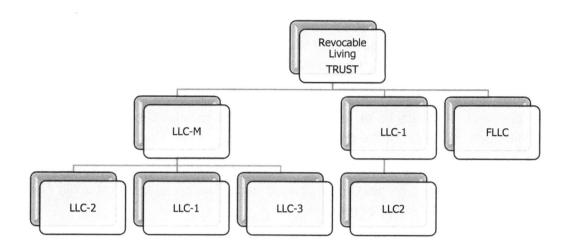

| STEP | DESCRIPTION |
|------|-------------|
| 1 | Set-up Revocable Living Trust (funded by LLCs) |
| 2 | Set-up FLLC |
| 3 | Purchase property under LLC-1 and LLC-2 |
| 4 | Open LLC-M as Master and place ownership of LLC-1 & 2 under it |
| 5 | Open up additional LLCs under LLC-M |

Federal Tax Attributes

- a Family Trust does not have to pay income tax on income that is distributed to the beneficiaries, but does have to pay tax on undistributed income

- the beneficiaries pay tax on the distributions made to them

## 10.4  Limited Liability Company (LLC)

The LLC offers the strongest asset protection for your business, replacing the Sub Chapter S as the corporate choice for all new business structures.  This form of asset protection compartmentalizes the asset and insulates you and your assets against potential liability.

The dreaded **Charging Order** can only be against LLC member(s) and not the LLC. (The "Charging Order" means that the (member) creditor has a right to all of the members' capital distributions.  When will you have a capital distribution?  **N E V E R**. You can take a salary, joint venture, borrow money, but NEVER take a capital distribution). The IRS in Revenue Ruling (77-137), stated that someone must pay taxes. Since the person holding the Charging Order will receive the K-1, they must pay the taxes on the income generated by the LLC, even though your creditor never receives any actual cash from the business. The judgment creditor is treated as a substituted limited partner for tax purposes and will suffer the tax consequences without capacity to force payment, dissolution, or distribution. Wouldn't you as the creditor settle under these conditions?

Advantages of LLC's:

- Limited liability: Owners of a LLC have the liability protection of a corporation. The LLC exists as a separate entity like a corporation. Members cannot be held responsible for debts of the LLC unless they have signed a personal guarantee.

- Flexible profit distribution: LLC can split the profits anyway, they wish. Usually by percentage of ownership.

- Flow through taxation: All business profits, losses, and expenses flow through the LLC to the individual members. There is no double taxation.

Disadvantages of LLC's:

- Limited life: Dissolves when a member dies or undergoes bankruptcy.

## 10.5  Charitable Remainder Trusts (CRT)

The charitable remainder trust is an irrevocable trust. In this trust, the beneficiary is a nonprofit charity of your choice. You benefit from a reliable lifetime income stream, and you also receive a charitable deduction at the time the trust is established. Because a charitable remainder trust is exempt from capital gains, no tax is due when the asset is sold or when the remainder is donated to the charity. In the end, *a minimum of 10 percent of the original value must be left in the trust* to benefit the selected charity.

Since many people are not comfortable donating a major asset to charity at the expense of their heirs, there is a remedy for this. The charitable remainder trust can purchase a life insurance policy on the annuitant that is payable to the heirs. Effectively, the life insurance payoff becomes their inheritance.

Advantages of Charitable Remainder Trusts are:

- eliminates capital gains taxes on appreciated property

- creates a stream of income without the risk of triggering taxes, or default on installment sales

- provides a charitable tax deduction in the year it is established and funded

- removes highly appreciated property from the estate

- can fund a life insurance policy to provide heirs with a replacement inheritance

*Note: Charitable Remainder Trusts (CRT) should be designed by an attorney due to the long-term implications and irrevocability of the trust.*

The two most popular types of Charitable Remainder Trusts are:

**Charitable Remainder Annuity Trusts** (CRAT):  pays a fixed income each year corresponding to a percentage of the original investment (5% minimum to 50% maximum).  Income is paid each year regardless of how much the CRAT earns from its investments.  If investment returns are insufficient to provide the required income, principal will be used to pay the required amount.

**Charitable Remainder Unit Trusts** (CRUT):  the CRUT does not require that the principal be used to sustain the income stream.  However, the option is available.  The CRUT provides more flexibility in how income streams are paid. The CRUT may increase with inflation or may not pay the appropriate amount in some years.  Variations on how the CRUT can make payments include

- as a set percentage of the annual value of the trust (may include paying out principal)

- income only that does not pay anything if the trust does not obtain an income from investments.  Principal is not used to make annual income payments.  Provisions can be made to have missed income made up in future years

**Charitable Remainder Trusts Taxes**
Capital gains tax is deferred until the beneficiary receives payments from the CRT and the taxes are slowly paid with inflated dollars.  Because the CRT continues to invest and generate earnings, the tax components in the CRT payment can be complex.  The CRT can be expected to earn a combination of tax-exempt income and taxable income.  The CRT does not pay taxes itself; you the beneficiary pay them.  The components of the payments you can expect are

- ordinary income

- tax-exempt income

- capital gains tax

- return of principal

*Note: the proportion in each year's payments will vary because of changing returns of investment in each category from year to year.*

## CHARITABLE OPTIONS COMPARISON

Charitable Remainder Annuity Trust

- Objective:  Fixed and potentially increases income

- Action Needed:  Establish a charitable trust with property or other assets

- General Benefits:  Immediate income tax deduction and fixed income for life

Charitable Remainder Unit Trust

- Objective:  Protect principal with varying income stream

- Action Needed:  Establish a trust that pays a percentage of the trust's assets; income varies

- General Benefits:  Immediate income tax deduction; annual income for life with potential to increases

Wealth Replacement Trust

- Objective:  Provides inheritance

- Action Needed:  Use increased income or tax deduction to fund life insurance policy

- General Benefits:  Heirs receive life insurance payout instead of property

Charitable Lead Trust

- Objective:  Reduce gift and estate taxes on assets planned for heirs

- Action Needed:  Create a trust that pays a fixed or variable income to charity for a set term and then passes to heirs

- General Benefits:  Reduced size of taxable estate; retains property in the family, often with reduced gift taxes

Retained Life Estate

- Objective:  Gift personal residence with lifetime right of use

- Action Needed:  Transfer title for home to charity, but retain occupancy

- General Benefits:  Current income tax deduction with charity obtaining residence upon death

Charitable Gift Annuity

- Objective:  Income with fixed annual payments from a contract rather than a trust

- Action Needed:  Gift to charity in exchange for contractual payments

- General Benefits:  Immediate and future savings on income taxes; fixed payments for life

Pooled Income Fund

- Objective:  Improved income from low rate of return property

- Action Needed:  Commingle property or other assets with other donors

- General Benefits:  Current income tax deduction; possible income improvement

# SECTION 11      THE HOME OFFICE

## 11.0  According to the IRS

Employees and self-employed individuals are permitted to deduct for a Home Office if the office is exclusively used on a regular basis under any of the following conditions:

- The office is used by the taxpayer for administrative or management activities of the taxpayer's trade or business.

- There is no other fixed location of the trade or business where the taxpayer conducts substantial administrative or management activities of the trade or business.

- If a self-employed taxpayer maintains an office in the home, the expenses are deductible for AGI.

Deduction and Limitations for the home office expenses are computed using the following two categories of expense:

- Expenses directly related to the office

  Direct expenses include operating expenses (supplies, etc.) that are used in the business as well as other expenses that relate solely to the office such as painting and decorating just the office.

- Expenses indirectly related to the office

  Indirect expenses are the prorated share (based on square foot) of expenses that benefit the entire house or apartment, such as mortgage interest (or rent), real estate taxes, insurance, utilities, and maintenance.

## 11.1  Virtual Addresses

Locate a local Mailbox Rental - Receiving and Forwarding Service Company and obtain a mailbox from them.  Use the box number as a *suite* so that you can receive all of your mail and packages there.  Another reason for this is YOU DO NOT WANT JUST ANYONE STROLLING UP TO YOUR FRONT DOOR.  This type of service can be found at Mr. Mailbox, Mail Depot, The UPS Store, etc.

Your business address, check, and other stationary should read:

ABC LLC
123 Main Street - Suite 56
Anywhere, CT 12345

If you are going to have your tenant base mail checks to you, consider opening a PO Box at the local Post Office just for that purpose.

## 11.2  Home Set-Up

Designate a room in your home that you can use exclusively for work.  The room should contain the following items at a minimum:

- Four (4) draw legal lateral file cabinet.

- Six (6) foot laminate kitchen counter (can be purchased at Home Depot).

- Three (3) two draw legal file cabinets.

- Large bookcase (solid wood 84"H x 36" W x 11 1/2" D w/6 shelves (4 adjustable).

- Work Desk (solid wood 72' x 30" x 30" D).

- Computer and Monitor.

  Software:  Microsoft Office Professional; Adobe Acrobat Pro; Symantec Norton 360.  All, the latest version.

- DYMO Label Writer Twin Turbo.

- Multi-Function Color Printer.

## 11.3  Internet

Secure a fast internet connection from your local ISP.  Once acquired the following should be connected after the company's modem:

- Cisco wireless security router with VPN - enhanced firewall, encryption and authentication features.

- Netgear PROSAFE 24PT GB smart switch.

## 11.4  File Folders

Purchase colored legal pressboard classification folders with partitions.  Set up folder as follows:

Property Research

- Inside Front Cover (*Property Research Table*)

- Front Partition (*APOD*)

- Back Partition (*TOWS Analysis*)

- Front Partition

- Back Partition

- Inside Back cover

  The tab should read as follows:  County, State

Investment Property

- Inside Front Cover

- Front Partition

- Back Partition

- Front Partition

- Back Partition

- Inside Back cover

  The tab should read as follows:

  Property Name, Address, City, Zip

*Originals of all Investment Properties, Closing Folders, and Tenant Folders documents including Building Plans to be kept in the vault.*


Closing Folder

- Inside Front Cover (*Copy of Original Leases*)

- Front Partition (*Copy of Insurance Policies*)

- Back Partition (*Copies of Existing Service Contracts; Name and Phone Numbers of Service People Being Used*)

- Front Partition (*Copy of Bill of Sale for Personal Property*)

- Back Partition (*Copy Closing Statement; Certificate of no Liens*)

- Inside Back cover (*Copy of Property Deed*)

  The tab should read as follows:

  County


Tenant Folder

- Inside Front Cover (*Event List*)

- Front Partition (*Correspondence*)

- Back Partition (*Appliances*)

- Front Partition (*Walk-Thru*)

- Back Partition (*References, Application*)

- Inside Back cover (*Signed Lease*)

    The tab should read as follows:

    County

    State


## 11.5  Standard Property File Labels

All properties managed should have files that include the standard labels listed below. Additional files should be added as appropriate.


Acquisition and Takeover

- Appraisal

- Correspondence

    Owner, Takeover

- Legal

- Management Agreement

- Management Plan

- Property Takeover

- Real Estate Closing


Administration

- Correspondence (various files as necessary)

- Employee

    Applications, Current (by employee), Past, Job Descriptions, Miscellaneous

- Forms (samples and form management files)

- Insurance

    Property, Employee, Claims

- Inventory (furniture, materials and supplies)

- Keys and Key Control

- Legal

  Resident, Other

- Licenses and Permits

- On-site Office

- Organization

- Reporting Schedule / Information

- Security

- Taxes

  Real Estate, Sales, Other


## Managing the Physical Asset

- Correspondence – Maintenance

- Capital Improvements

- Inspections

- Maintenance

  Corrective, Custodial, Deferred, Emergency, Preventive

- Service Contracts (file for each contractor or contract type)

- Maintenance Detail Files (as appropriate, e.g. air conditioning, appliances, carpet, ceilings, doors, electrical, elevators, energy, floor, foundation, gas, halls, heating, janitorial, landscape, lighting, mailboxes, parking lot, pest control, plumbing, remodeling and repairs, roof, shop, signs, sprinkler system, stairs, supplies, trash removal, water and sewer, utilities, walls, windows and window cleaning).


## Marketing and Leasing

- Advertising

- Brochures

- Commissions

- Floor Plans

- Lease Form(s)

- Leasing Policy and Procedures

- Lease - Legal

- Marketing Plan /Studies

- Photographs

- Promotions

- Public Relations

- Signs

## Tenant Management

- Apartment Unit Details

- Collection Procedures

- Correspondence – Residents

- Eviction Procedures

- Move-in / Move-out Information

- Other Income

- Rent Rolls

- Resident Associations

- Resident Lease / Files (one for each apartment unit)

- Resident Ledgers (one for each resident / unit)

- Resident Lists

- Resident Relations

- Security Deposit Schedule

## Financial Management

- Accounting and Bookkeeping (various files as appropriate)

- Banking

- Budgets

- Cash Flow Statements

- Chart of Accounts

- Correspondence – Financial

- Comparative Statements

- Financing (including mortgage information)

- Management Fee

- Operating Statements

- Paid and Unpaid Bills

- Purchasing – Vendor List

# SECTION 12    THE BUSINESS PLAN

The following is a sample list of what should be included in your business plan, please expand.

## 1.0    Company Description

### 1.1    Overview

The ABC LLC is a new start-up company managed by its start-up team.  John Doe and Jane Doe.

### 1.2    Members

John Doe, will manage the over-all operations of the company as its Asset Manager. John is a graduate of Hard Knocks University, and has 10 years in Restaurant Management.

Jane Doe, will manage the company's bookkeeping.  Jane has 4 year experience as a bookkeeper.

### 1.3    Company Classification

North American Industry Classification System (NAICS);

Division H:              Real Estate

Major Group 65:         Real Estate

Industry Group 651      Real Estate Operators and Lessors.

### 1.4    Objectives

A. ABC LLC intends to purchase and manage Multifamily Housing in suburban and urban areas.  These Housing Communities will offer the Residents (tenants) a safe haven to live and raise their children.

B. The objectives of ABC LLC are to generate a profit, grow at a challenging rate, and to create a family portfolio of commercial residential properties.

C. To provide for retirement and family inheritance. Property appreciation, and principal reduction now, passive income during retirement, and then to pass-on the portfolio tax-free to my heirs.

## 1.5    Mission

A. To provide a basis for a family business.

B. To purchase and manage (through our Resident Managers) small commercial residential properties (5-125 units).

C. To eventually move up to large commercial residential community properties, which will be professionally managed.

D. To achieve all short-term and long-term objectives.

## 1.6    Services and Strategies

Our principal service will consist of renting residential real estate in our targeted market areas.

A. To use maximum leverage to obtain objectives.

B. To hire competent Independent Contractors (tradespeople) to complement the Residential Manager in sustaining the properties, and the performance of the building systems. As a Team Member, the tradespeople will sustain the building's overall profitability by addressing resident comfort, equipment reliability, and efficient operation.

## 2.0    Market Analysis and Plan

## 2.1    Management Planning

A. To provide asset management.

B. To provide for general maintenance planning.

C. To plan for long term capital maintenance.

D. To provide property operating budgets.

E. To analyze comparables to determine rental pricing.

**2.2   Marketing Services**

A. To provide local advertising (local yellow pages, newspaper ads, etc.)

B. To customize the rental listing.

C. To put up signage along with marketing literature at property.

D. To utilize multiple internet sites to promote prospects.

**3.0   Target Market**

**3.1   Leasing Services**

A. To screen prospective applicants and show properties.

B. To provide thorough application processing including:

   a. Credit Report;

   b. Employment Verification and History;

   c. Landlord Verification and Reference; and

   d. Criminal Background Check.

C. To collect security and pet deposit as applicable.

D. To execute Leasing Agreement

E. To coordinate occupancy, and arrange for possession and keys.

**3.2   Analysis of Investment Threats, Opportunities, Weaknesses and Strengths**

Complete the TOWS Analysis chart for your farm area.

**4.0   Competition**

Use your TOWS to answer this slot.

**5.0    Competitive Strategy**

Use your market analysis and TOWS to answer this slot.

**6.0    Management Team**

**6.1    Officers**

CEO            , Member

Secretary      , Member

Treasurer      , Member

**6.2    Advisors**

Attorney

Accountant

Bank Officer

**6.3    Team Members**

Resident Manager

Plumber

Electrician

Landscaper

Glass Technician

**7.0    Startup and Growth Plan**

**7.1    Entry**

A. The types of property you are looking for (5-25 units; 25-50; units 51-100 unit; 101 or more).

B. The price range you are considering.

C. The holding period (2-5 years).

**7.2    Post-Entry**

A.  Management changes (will you manage the community yourself, have a Resident Manager or employ a Property Management Company).

B.  Property improvements.

C.  Rental increases (what determines when a rent increase is required?  Market, improvements, other influences, or a combination of all of these factors).

**7.3    Exit Strategy**

A.  Short term retention or long term wealth accumulation.

B.  Estimate tax liability.

C.  Cash flow or property enhancement.

D.  Refinancing (it takes 12 months for a property to season).

E.  Trade-up or sell.

**8.0    Technology Plan**

**8.1    Computerized Advertising.**

A.  Upload vacancy information (including photo) to the web.

B.  Send vacancy information to Google, Zillow, Trulia, Oodle and Craigslist.

C.  Create flyers.

**8.2    Computerized Accounting procedures**

A.  Deposit accounting.

B.  Monthly accounting statements.

C.  Income and expense by category and year to date figures.

D.  Year-end statement recaps and breakdown.

E.  1099 preparation for tax purposes.

**8.3    Online Banking**

   A.  Receive rent payments online 24 hours a day, 7 days a week.

   B.  Major credit card acceptance.

   C.  Vendor payments.

**8.4    Tenant Files**

   A.  Separate ledgers with easy access.

   B.  Automatic posting.

   C.  Detailed Property features.

   D.  Vendor information.

   E.  Easy check writing.

   F.  Point and click reports.

**8.5    Miscellaneous Functions**

   A.  Back-up.

   B.  Reports.

**9.0    Financial Plan or Forecast (5 years or more)**

**9.1    Startup Budget (Sample)**

|  | **CASH NEEDED TO START** | **% of TOTAL** |
|---|---|---|
| **Management** |  |  |
| Advertising | 1,800.00 | .45% |
| Auto & Travel | 500.00 | .125% |
| Insurance | 3,000.00 | .75% |
| Resident Manager | 1.200.00 | .30% |
| Supplies | 500.00 | .125% |
| *subtotal* | **$7,000.00** | **1.75%** |
| **Legal/Accounting** |  |  |
| Accounting | 5,000.00 | 1.25% |
| Legal | 5,000.00 | 1.25% |

| | | |
|---|---|---|
| *subtotal* | **$10,000.00** | **2.50%** |
| **Miscellaneous** | | |
| Grounds | 5,000.00 | 1.25% |
| Pest Control | 1,000.00 | .25% |
| Repairs | 2,000.00 | .50% |
| Stationary | 400.00 | .10% |
| Supplies | 600.00 | .15% |
| *subtotal* | **$9,000.00** | **2.25%** |
| **Taxes** | | |
| Real Estate | 40,000.00 | 10.00% |
| Personal Property | 200.00 | .05% |
| Payroll | 200.00 | .05% |
| Other | 600.00 | .15% |
| *subtotal* | **$41,000.00** | **10.25%** |
| **Utilities** | | |
| Electricity | 1,500.00 | .37% |
| Gas | 2,000.00 | .50% |
| Fuel Oil | 2,000.00 | .50% |
| Water | 2,000.00 | .50% |
| Sewer | 2,000.00 | .50% |
| Trash Removal | 3,000.00 | .75% |
| Telephone | 1,000.00 | .25% |
| Miscellaneous | 3,500.00 | .88% |
| *subtotal* | **$18,000.00** | **4.50%** |
| **Consultants** | | |
| Appraiser | 5,000.00 | 1.25% |
| Other | 10,000.00 | 2.50% |
| *subtotal* | **$15,000.00** | **3.75%** |
| **Funding** | | |
| Investment #1 | 100,000.00 | 25.00% |
| Investment #2 | 100,000.00 | 25.00% |
| Miscellaneous | 50,000.00 | 12.50% |
| *subtotal* | **$250,000.00** | **62.50%** |
| **Checking** | | |
| Disbursement | 25,000.00 | 6.25% |
| Trust Money Market | 1,000.00 | .25% |
| Purchase Account | 24,000.00 | 6.00% |
| *subtotal* | **$50,000.00** | **12.50%** |
| | | |
| | **$400,000.00** | **100%** |

Start-up $400,000.00. If more is available, adjust for percentages given above. Miscellaneous items under Management, Legal/Accounting, Taxes, Utilities, and Consultants should be kept in the disbursement account until needed.

## 10.0   Miscellaneous

Add in items as recommended by your professional (attorney, accountant) team members.

# APPENDIX A

## SAMPLE FORMS, CHARTS and LETTERS

| MANAGEMENT | FIGURE | FORM | DESCRIPTION |
|---|---|---|---|
| **OWNER** | | | |
| Ownership | OMA-1 | COO | Change of Ownership Meeting |
| | OMA-2 | NOL | New Ownership Letter |
| | OMA-3 | LTM | List of Team Members |
| Back Office | OMB-1 | CIF | Capital Improvements |
| | OMB-2 | UDD | Unit Due Diligence |
| | OMB-3 | PLF | Phone Log |
| | OMB-4 | TSF | Traffic Sheet |
| | OMB-5 | SPL | Sample Presentation |
| | OMB-6 | TAF | Tenant Application Checklist |
| | OMB-7 | RLF | Chart of Outstanding Rents and Late Fees |
| | OMB-8 | MOC | Move-out Checklist (office) |
| | OMB-9 | SFL | Standard File Labels |
| | OMB-10 | OHF | Prospect from Open House |
| Pre-Lease | OMP-1 | PAL | Application Information |
| | OMP-2 | HDF | Holding Deposit Receipt |
| | OMP-3 | NCL | Non-Bias Criteria Checklist |
| | OMP-4 | LLV | Landlord Verification |
| | OMP-5 | TVL | Prospect Resident Verification |
| | OMP-6 | EVR | Employment Verification |
| | OMP-7 | ATR | Application to Rent |
| | OMP-8 | PGU | Personal Guarantor |
| Lease | OML-1 | LGA | Letter of Acceptance |
| | OML-2 | AGL | Acceptance Letter with Lease Agreement |
| | OML-3 | MPA | Month-to-Month Pet Agreement |
| | OML-4 | PAC | Pet Agreement |
| | OML-5 | TMB | Tenant Move-in Checklist |
| | OML-6 | DRA | Document Receipt Acknowledgement |
| | OML-7 | WNR | Welcome New Resident |
| | OML-8 | FORM | House Rules and Policies |
| | OML-9 | FORM | Tenant Lease |
| Termination | OMT-1 | CDF | Collection Detail and Checklist |
| | OMT-2 | NAL | Non-Acceptance Letter |
| | OMT-3 | NLA | Notice of Abandonment |
| | OMT-4 | NOT | Notice of Termination Letter |
| | OMT-5 | NRL | Non-Renewable of Lease |
| | | | |
| | | | |
| | | | |
| | | | |
| | | | |
| | | | |
| | | | |

| TENANT | | | |
|---|---|---|---|
| General | TMG-1 | MKF | Master Key Log |
| | TMG-2 | NIE | Notice of Intent to Enter Dwelling Unit |
| | TMG-3 | RSF | Request for Service |
| | TMG-4 | TEL | Tenant Exit Letter |
| | TMG-5 | GLF | Guide-lines for Return of Security |
| | TMG-6 | TEL | Tenant Exit Letter |
| | TMG-7 | EIF | Resident Exit Interview |
| Performance | TMP-1 | BCL | Bad Check Letter |
| | TMP-2 | TWE | Rent Late Warning and Excuses |
| | TMP-3 | PAR | Payment Applies to Arrears |
| | TMP-4 | NPL | Non-Performance Letter to Bureau |
| | TMP-5 | RDA | Resident Damage Letter |
| | TMP-6 | IRF | Incident Report |
| | TMP-7 | UOL | Use and Occupancy |
| | TMP-8 | LRN | Notice |
| Receivables | TMR-1 | AML | Pay Rent in Arrears |
| | TMR-2 | RIL | Rent Increase Letter |
| | TMR-3 | SDA | Security Deposit Accounting |
| | TMR-4 | RRR | Residential Rent Roll |

Figure OMA-1

## Sample: **Change of Ownership Meeting — Form COO**

*<< Date >>*

Dear *<< Resident >>*;

We hope that you received our welcome letter, informing you of the change of ownership. As the Landlord, I would like to set-up an appointment to personally meet with you and your family, and to:

1.      Review the condition of your home. This is an opportune time for you to inform me of any problems, complaints, or positive statements that you may have.

2.      To put aside any fears that you may have, about your current rental agreement. Your current rent is applicable until the expiration date noted in the old agreement.

3.      To inform you that your old landlord has turned over your security deposit to us. We would like to verify the amount you provided against our records.

4.      We would also like to use this opportunity to update your contact information including emergency contacts and telephone numbers.

5.      State law requires us to have a copy of the keys that work in your locks. We will verify that the keys that we received at closing work in your lock. If for any reason, they were changed, please arrange to have the proper key for us at that time. *This is required by state law!*

6.      To inform you of electronic transfers, and how they can save you time and money in paying your rent.

We have set aside the next two weeks, Monday through Friday 5:00 PM until 8:00 PM, Saturday 10:00 AM till 6:00 PM. If this schedule does not work, please call and we will schedule a convenient time.

As the Landlord, I am strongly concerned about the current and future state of the property and all its attachments. I will provide you with my contact information so that you can contact me with any concerns that you may have.

Sincerely,

_____

*<< Landlord >>|<< Asset Manager >>*

Figure OMA-2

Sample:  **New Ownership Letter – Form NOL**

*<< Date >>*

To: *<< Mr. Tenant >>* and *<< Mrs. Tenant >>*

Dear Resident:

We are pleased to announce that ABC LLC has purchased the property that you are residing in. Please note the information listed below.

|  |  |
|---:|:---|
| Property Owner: | *<<Property Owner >>* |
| Office Phone: | *<< Office Phone >>* |
| Make Rent Checks Payable to: | *<< Payment to Company >>* |
| Mail Checks to: | *<< Mail Checks To >>* |

If you have any questions about this information, please call the Property Owner.

We welcome your comments and suggestions to aid our efforts in offering you the finest management service.  We look forward to a long and mutually beneficial relationship.

Sincerely,

_____

*<< Landlord >>, <<Property Owner >>*

Figure OMA-3

Sample: **List of Team Members – Form LTM**

| TEAM MEMBERS | | | | | | |
|---|---|---|---|---|---|---|
| | | PHONE | NAME | BUSINESS NAME | ADDRESS | NOTES |
| **Accounting** | | | | | | |
| Accountant | | | | | | |
| **Legal** | | | | | | |
| Attorney | | | | | | |
| **Appliances** | | | | | | |
| Repair Service | | | | | | |
| | | | | | | |
| **Exterior** | | | | | | |
| Chimney | | | | | | |
| Landscaping | | | | | | |
| Paint | | | | | | |
| Roofing | | | | | | |
| Window Replacement | | | | | | |
| **Environmental** | | | | | | |
| Asbestos | | | | | | |
| Lead Abatement | | | | | | |
| Mold | | | | | | |
| Pest Control | | | | | | |
| | | | | | | |
| **Interior** | | | | | | |
| Burglar Alarm | | | | | | |
| Dry Wall | | | | | | |
| Electric | | | | | | |
| HVAC | | | | | | |
| Locksmith | | | | | | |
| Paint | | | | | | |
| Plumbing | | | | | | |

Figure OMB-1

Sample: **Capital Improvements – Form CIF**

| CAPITAL IMPROVEMENTS | | | | |
|---|---|---|---|---|
| SYSTEM | PROBLEM | CONTRACTOR | ESTIMATE | SUB-TOTAL |
| | | | | |
| Structural | | | | |
| | | | | |
| | | | | |
| | | | | |
| | | | TOTAL = | $ |
| HVAC | | | | |
| | | | | |
| | | | | |
| | | | | |
| | | | | |
| | | | | |
| | | | TOTAL = | $ |
| Plumbing | | | | |
| | | | | |
| | | | | |
| | | | | |
| | | | | |
| | | | | |
| | | | TOTAL = | $ |
| Sprinkler | | | | |
| | | | | |
| | | | TOTAL = | $ |
| Electrical | | | | |
| | | | | |
| | | | | |
| | | | | |
| | | | | |
| | | | TOTAL = | $ |
| Other | | | | |
| | | | | |
| | | | | |
| | | | | |
| | | | TOTAL = | $ |

Figure OMB-2

Sample: **Unit Due Diligence – Form UDD**

| | UNIT DUE DILIGENCE REPORT | | | | |
|---|---|---|---|---|---|
| **Property Name:** | | | | | |
| Address: _____ | | | Unit: _____ | | |
| City: _____ | | State: _____ | Zip:_____ | | |

| ITEM | DESCRIPTION | GOOD | CONDITION AVERAGE | POOR | COMMENT |
|---|---|---|---|---|---|
| **1** | **Bathroom** | | | | |
| | Cabinets | | | | |
| | Ceiling | | | | |
| | Exhaust Fan | | | | |
| | Floor | | | | |
| | Paint | | | | |
| | Sink(s) / Trim | | | | |
| | Tile | | | | |
| | Toilet | | | | |
| | Tub/Shower | | | | |
| | Vanity | | | | |
| | Shower Door / Curtain Rod | | | | |
| | | | | | |
| **2** | **Bedroom 1** | | | | |
| | Ceiling | | | | |
| | Closet | | | | |
| | Blinds | | | | |
| | Door | | | | |
| | Floor/Carpet | | | | |
| | Paint | | | | |
| | Windows | | | | |
| | Comfort Unit (heat-a/c) | | | | |
| | | | | | |
| **3** | **Bedroom 2** | | | | |
| | Ceiling | | | | |
| | Closet | | | | |

| | | | | |
|---|---|---|---|---|
| Blinds | | | | |
| Door | | | | |
| Floor/Carpet | | | | |
| Paint | | | | |
| Windows | | | | |
| | | | | |

| **4** | **Bedroom 3** | | | |
|---|---|---|---|---|
| Ceiling | | | | |
| Closet | | | | |
| Blinds | | | | |
| Door | | | | |
| Paint | | | | |
| Floor/Carpet | | | | |
| Windows | | | | |
| Comfort Unit (heat-a/c) | | | | |
| | | | | |
| | | | | |

| **5** | **Kitchen** | | | |
|---|---|---|---|---|
| Cabinets | | | | |
| Ceiling | | | | |
| Closet | | | | |
| Counters | | | | |
| Blinds | | | | |
| Dishwasher | | | | |
| Door | | | | |
| Paint | | | | |
| Floor / Tile | | | | |
| Refrigerator | | | | |
| Sink / Trim | | | | |
| Stove | | | | |
| Windows | | | | |
| Comfort Unit (heat-a/c) | | | | |
| | | | | |
| Entry Door | | | | |
| Water Heater | | | | |
| | | | | |
| Smoke Detectors | | | | |

| | Carbon Dioxide Detector | | | | |
|---|---|---|---|---|---|
| | | | | | |
| | | | | | |

| 7 | Tenant Comments |
|---|---|
| | |

| 8 | Miscellaneous Notes |
|---|---|
| | |
| | |
| | |
| | |
| | |
| | |

Figure OMB-3

Sample: **Phone Log – Form PLF**

## Phone Log

**MEDIA: Yellow Pages (YP); Web (W); Resident Manager (RM) who/where**

| MEDIA | NAME | TELEPHONE | BR | BA | WHEN |
|-------|------|-----------|----|----|------|
| | | | | | |
| | | | | | |
| | | | | | |
| | | | | | |
| | | | | | |
| | | | | | |
| | | | | | |
| | | | | | |
| | | | | | |
| | | | | | |
| | | | | | |
| | | | | | |
| | | | | | |
| | | | | | |
| | | | | | |
| | | | | | |
| | | | | | |
| | | | | | |
| | | | | | |
| | | | | | |
| | | | | | |
| | | | | | |
| | | | | | |
| | | | | | |
| | | | | | |
| | | | | | |
| | | | | | |
| | | | | | |
| | | | | | |

Figure OMB-4

Sample:  **Traffic Sheet – Form TSF**

## Traffic Sheet

| PROSECT | CURRENT ADDRESS | TELEPHONE | BR | BA | WHEN |
|---------|-----------------|-----------|----|----|------|
|  |  |  |  |  |  |
|  |  |  |  |  |  |
|  |  |  |  |  |  |
|  |  |  |  |  |  |
|  |  |  |  |  |  |
|  |  |  |  |  |  |
|  |  |  |  |  |  |
|  |  |  |  |  |  |
|  |  |  |  |  |  |
|  |  |  |  |  |  |
|  |  |  |  |  |  |
|  |  |  |  |  |  |
|  |  |  |  |  |  |
|  |  |  |  |  |  |
|  |  |  |  |  |  |
|  |  |  |  |  |  |
|  |  |  |  |  |  |
|  |  |  |  |  |  |
|  |  |  |  |  |  |
|  |  |  |  |  |  |
|  |  |  |  |  |  |
|  |  |  |  |  |  |
|  |  |  |  |  |  |
|  |  |  |  |  |  |
|  |  |  |  |  |  |
|  |  |  |  |  |  |
|  |  |  |  |  |  |
|  |  |  |  |  |  |
|  |  |  |  |  |  |

Figure OMB-5

Sample: **Sample Presentation – Form SPL**

## SAMPLE PRESENTATION

The Resident Manager should be able to answer the following questions, or to make it part of his presentation to a prospective Resident.

| INDEX | SUBJECT AREA | QUESTION |
|-------|--------------|----------|
| A | Apartment | What is the square footage of the apartment? <br> When is the rent due? <br> When can I move in? <br> Can I move in early? |
| A | Amenities | Does the property have a washer and dryer?  How much does it cost? <br> Is there a dishwasher? <br> Can I get cable/satellite? <br> Can I get Internet access? |
| M | Parking | Is there parking? |
| P | Pets | Do you allow pets? <br> How much is the pet deposit? |
| S | Smoking | Is the property nonsmoking? |
| T | Transportation | Is it close to public transportation? |
| U | | Are utilities included? <br> What are the average utility bills? |

The Resident Manager should ask interested prospects the following questions before (telephone) or when they are at an open house.

| INDEX | SUBJECT AREA | QUESTION |
|-------|--------------|----------|
| A | Apartment | Where are you living now? <br> What date are you looking to move? |
| A | Amenities | |
| | Parking | |
| P | Pets | Do you have any pets? |
| R | Rent | The rent is $xxxxxxx a month.  Is that your price range? |
| R | Resident | Why are you moving? <br> How many people would be moving in? <br> Do you have any roommates? <br> Do you or your roommates/family members' smoke? |

Figure OMB-6

Sample: **Tenant Application Checklist – Form TAF**

## Tenant Application Checklist

Property:                                        Applicant(s):

_____

_____

Reviewed by: _____     Move-in Date: _____     Apt: _____

Application Checklist must be completed for all applications. Answers on the application must be confirmed by credit check and with applicant's employer, landlord, etc. Responses, agreements, and discrepancies should be noted as appropriate on the application. Checklist must be used in conjunction with the Move-in Checklist.

|  |  | By | Date |
|---|---|---|---|
| 1. | Completed application received | ____ | _____ |
| 1a. | Photo of applicant and co-applicant | ____ | _____ |
| 2. | Application and deposit fees received | ____ | _____ |
| 3. | Impressions of applicant based on interview: | ____ | _____ |

_____

_____

4.     Bank reference obtained                                        ____   _____

   a. Accounts opened:                    $ _____

   b. Checking balance/range:             $ _____

   c. Savings balance/range:              $ _____

   d. Ask if there are any bank loans outstanding.

   Contact: _____     Title:

                                     _____

   Contact: _____     Title:

                                     _____

5.     Credit check completed. Agency:                             ____   _____

   _____

For each credit reference, ask the
following:

    a. What is the amount of outstanding balance?

    b. What is the minimum monthly payment?

    c. Does applicant pay on time?

    d. What is the amount of credit line?

    e. What is the rating?

6.    Employment verified (prior two years)    _____  _____

    a. Ask about likelihood of continued employment.

    Contact: _____    Title:

                                                      _____

    Contact: _____    Title:

                                                      _____

7.    Spouse's employment verified    _____  _____

    a. Ask about likelihood of continued employment.

    Contact: _____    Title:

                                                       _____

    Contact: _____    Title:

                                                      _____

8.    Housing verified (prior two years)    _____  _____

    a. Ask prior landlords: Would you rent to applicant again?

    ☐ Yes ☐ No If no, ask for an explanation.

    b. Did applicant pay on time? ☐ Yes ☐ No

    Contact: _____    Title:

                                                       _____

    Contact: _____    Title:

                                                      _____

9.    Personal references called (if necessary)    _____  _____

    _____

    _____

10.    Income qualification summary/analysis    _____  _____

| **Monthly Payments** | | Gross Monthly Income | |
|---|---|---|---|
| Bank loan(s) | $ _____ | Applicant | $ _____ |
| Auto loan(s) | $ _____ | Spouse | $ _____ |
| Credit card(s) | $ _____ | Total | $ _____ |
| Other | $ _____ | | |
| **Subtotal** | $ _____ | ____% | |
| Add: Rent | $ _____ | ____% | *of total gross monthly income* |
| **Total** | $ _____ | ____% | |

*If sum of rent and monthly payments exceed Total Gross Monthly income (or 28 percent of Gross Monthly Income), application is rejected; if percentage of rent and monthly payments is less than 33 percent of gross monthly incomes, application may be approved subject to information on other portions of the application.*

11. Application meets minimum income requirements. ☐ Yes ☐ No
If no, reject application. ____ _____

12. Verification letter(s) mailed: ☐ Employment ____ _____
☐ Credit
☐ Residence

13. Verification letter(s) returned: ☐ Employment ____ _____
☐ Credit
☐ Residence

14. Evaluation: ☐ Approve ☐ Disapprove ____ _____

15. Application and Checklist reviewed by: ____ _____

16. Prospect notified of approval/rejection ____ _____

Notes:

Figure OMB-7

Sample: **Chart of Outstanding Rents and Late Fees – Form RLF**

| CHART OF OUTSTANDING RENTS & LATE FEES | | | | | |
|---|---|---|---|---|---|
| Date | Tenant | Unit | Late Rent | Late Fee | Comments |
|  |  |  |  |  |  |
|  |  |  |  |  |  |
|  |  |  |  |  |  |
|  |  |  |  |  |  |
|  |  |  |  |  |  |

Figure OMB-8

Sample: **Move-out Checklist – Form MOC**

# MOVE-OUT CHECKLIST (office)

Property:                                          Unit:


Resident:                          Move Out Date:


| | | By | Date |
|---|---|---|---|
| 1. | Written notice to vacate. | | |
| 2. | Appointment to meet with resident: | | |
| | Date:                    Time: | | |
| 3. | Monies due determined from resident ledger card. | | |
| 4. | Met with resident. | | |
| | • Discussed reason(s) for vacating. | | |
| | • Exit interview completed. | | |
| | • Arrangements made for showing apartment. | | |
| 5. | Move-out procedures discussed. | | |
| | • Rent paid in full. | | |
| | • Unit cleaned. | | |
| | • Damages if any repaired. | | |
| 6. | Pre-move inspection made. | | |
| 7. | Unit posted to Vacancy Report. | | |
| 8. | Move-out inspection completed, signed by resident. | | |
| 9. | Forwarding address obtained. | | |
| 10. | Security deposit accounting completed. | | |
| | • Security deposit accounting presented to resident. | | |
| | • Refund made, if any. | | |
| 11. | Outstanding balances collected, if any. | | |
| 12. | Name removed from mailbox and directory. | | |
| 13. | Make-ready checklist prepared. | | |
| 14. | Keys returned. | | |
| 15. | Resident files updated and placed in inactive file. | | |

Notes:

Figure OMB-9

Sample: **Standard File Labels – Form SFL**

## Standard Property File Labels

All properties managed should have files that include the standard labels listed below. Additional files should be added as appropriate.

| **Administration** | | |
|---|---|---|
| ☐ | Correspondence (various files as necessary) | |
| ☐ | Forms (samples and form management files) | |
| ☐ | Insurance | |
| | • | Property |
| | • | Employee |
| | • | Claims |
| ☐ | Inventory (furniture, materials and supplies) | |
| ☐ | Keys and Key Control | |
| ☐ | Legal | |
| | • | Resident |
| | • | Other |
| ☐ | Licenses and Permits | |
| ☐ | On-site Office | |
| ☐ | Organization | |
| ☐ | Reporting Schedule/Information | |
| ☐ | Security | |
| **Managing the Physical Asset** | | |
| ☐ | Correspondence - Maintenance | |
| ☐ | Capital Improvements | |
| ☐ | Inspections | |
| ☐ | Maintenance | |
| | • | Corrective |
| | • | Custodial |
| | • | Deferred |
| | • | Emergency |
| | • | Preventive |
| ☐ | Service Contracts (file for each contractor or contract type) | |
| ☐ | Maintenance Detail Files (as appropriate, e.g. air conditioning, appliances, carpet, ceilings, doors, electrical, elevators, energy, floor, foundation, gas, halls, heating, janitorial, landscape, lighting, mailboxes, parking lot, pest control, plumbing, remodeling and repairs, roof, shop, signs, sprinkler system, stairs, supplies, trash removal, water and sewer, utilities, walls, windows and window cleaning.) | |
| ☐ | | |
| | | |

## Marketing and Leasing

| | | |
|---|---|---|
| ☐ | Advertising | |
| ☐ | Brochures | |
| ☐ | Floor Plans | |
| ☐ | Lease Form(s) | |
| ☐ | Leasing Policy and Procedures | |
| ☐ | Lease-Legal | |
| ☐ | Lease-Legal | |
| ☐ | Marketing Plan/Studies | |
| ☐ | Photographs | |
| ☐ | Promotions | |
| ☐ | Public Relations | |
| ☐ | Signs | |
| ☐ | | |
| ☐ | | |

## Tenant Management

| | | |
|---|---|---|
| ☐ | Apartment Unit Details | |
| ☐ | Collection Procedures | |
| ☐ | Correspondence - Residents | |
| ☐ | Eviction Procedures | |
| ☐ | Move-in/Move-out Information | |
| ☐ | Other Income | |
| ☐ | Rent Rolls | |
| | | |
| ☐ | Resident Leases/Files (one for each apartment unit) | |
| ☐ | Resident Ledgers (one for each resident/unit) | |
| ☐ | Resident Lists | |
| ☐ | Resident Relations | |
| ☐ | Security Deposit Schedule | |
| ☐ | | |
| ☐ | | |

## Financial Management

| | | |
|---|---|---|
| ☐ | Accounting and Bookkeeping (various files as appropriate) | |
| ☐ | Banking | |
| ☐ | Budgets | |
| ☐ | Cash Flow Statements | |
| ☐ | Chart of Accounts | |
| ☐ | Correspondence - Financial | |
| ☐ | Operating Statements | |
| ☐ | Paid and Unpaid Bills | |
| ☐ | Purchasing - Vendor List | |

Figure OMB-10

Sample: **Prospect from Open House – Form OHF**

Date: << *Date* >>

RE:   << *Address* >>
      << *City* >>, << *State* >> << *Zip* >>

Dear Prospective Tenant:

It was a pleasure meeting you at our rental home, and I am pleased that you are considering making it your new home.  We are enclosing for your review, additional information about our Community to help you make your decision.

I hope this information is of help to you, and we look forward to discussing your new home with you.  Please call if you have any additional questions.

We cannot hold our rental for you unless we hear from you soon!

Sincerely,

_____

<< *Asset Manager* >>

Figure OMP-1

Sample: **Application Information – Form PAL**

## Application Information

### or

## Preapplication and Notification

Dear Rental Applicant,

We take pride in our rental apartments, and we actively seek only qualified tenants to reside in them. We screen our applicants carefully, and we completely verify all information provided to us on the rental application. We run a credit report on every applicant as well as a criminal background check and employment verification, and we check previous rental history.

The screening and verification process is used for every applicant the same way—**fairly and consistently**. We are in compliance with the fair housing laws at all times. An applicant who passes the screening criteria is offered a tenancy when one is available. An applicant who does not satisfy the screening criteria is not accepted as a tenant. If there is more than one applicant for the same rental, the most qualified applicant will be accepted.

By making an application for one of our rentals, you acknowledge that these verifications will be completed and give us permission to do them. Please completely fill in the rental application. If you do not provide us with complete information, we will not be able to process the application. We will do our best to process your application quickly (normally within a seventy-two-hour period). If you have not heard back from us by then, feel free to contact us. Please read and sign below, acknowledging acceptance of the terms of your application. Thank you for making an application for one of our rentals, and we hope you will become a long-term resident with us.

1. I have double-checked the information I have provided on the rental application and agree that it is true and complete.

2. I understand that an annual update of the information on this application may be requested. I agree to provide updated information and notify management of any changes (i.e., employment, phone number, bank, car, emergency contact).

3. My credit report/history is good. If not, I have attached a separate page to explain my credit problems.

4. I understand and agree that this application is subject to approval based on the information on my application. If any of the information I have given turns out to be false, my application will be denied.

5. I understand and agree that this application is *not* a lease or rental agreement and, should it be accepted, I will sign the lease provided within five business days of being accepted. Should I fail to do so, the application shall be considered withdrawn. There will be no further obligation to reserve the rental, and my holding deposit will be forfeited.

6. I hereby waive any claim for damages if my application is not accepted.

7. I understand that every good-faith effort will be made to have the premises ready for occupancy as promised. However, should the premises not be available for occupancy on the date promised, I hereby waive any and all rights to seek to recover damages of any kind from the Landlord or Management Company.

8. I hereby authorize and permit the Landlord and/or Management Company to obtain any information necessary to verify the accuracy of any information or statements I have made on this application. I authorize and permit my credit report to be obtained and further authorize the Landlord or Management Company to make further credit inquires in regard to continued creditworthiness and for purposes of collection of unpaid rent or damages to premises, should that become necessary.

9. I permit, upon occasion, contact with my employer to verify my employment status during my tenancy.

10. I shall not hold the Landlord or Management Company responsible for any allergic reactions to the premises, inside or outside, from me, other occupants, or guests. I shall check for allergic reactions before signing the Lease Agreement.

11. I certify that I am not manufacturing, using, storing, or selling dangerous controlled substances and understand that I will immediately be required to vacate the premises if evidence of such is found on the premises or if I am convicted of any crimes related to possession and/or distribution of controlled, dangerous substances.

12. I further understand and agree that the security deposit and first month's rent must be paid in full by **money order** or **teller's check** before moving in. If I am unable to or fail for whatever reason to pay the balance of the amount due at that time, the application shall be considered withdrawn, and my holding deposit will be forfeited.


By: _____     _____     _____
      (applicant's signature)       (applicant to print name)      (date)


By: _____     _____     _____
      (applicant's signature)       (applicant to print name)      (date)

Figure OMP-2

Sample:  **Holding Deposit Receipt – Form HDF**

**Holding Deposit Receipt**

Applicant's Name:  << *Applicant Name* >>

Phone: << *Applicant's Phone* >>

Current Address: << *Applicant's Current Address* >>

<< *City* >>, << *State* >> << *Zip* >>

---

Property Address:
<< *Address* >>
<< *City* >>, << *State* >> << *Zip* >>

In the event the application for residency is not approved, or if the residence is not ready for occupancy, the deposit will be returned to the applicant.  If the applicant fails to sign the rental agreement, fails to provide additional funds required for occupancy, or does not take occupancy on the scheduled move-in date, $200.00 of this holding deposit will not be refunded to the applicant and will be retained by the owner/manager.

Rental Term:  ☐ lease from  _____ to _____

**Amount Deposited:**

Application fee $75.00      $ 75.00 non-refundable

Holding deposit      $200.00 (to be applied toward option consideration when lease is signed.)

**TOTAL:   $275.00 (monies received by cash _____ check # _____)**

**By signing below applicant acknowledges receipt of this notice.**

---

Today's Date:  _____ 20_____

Anticipated Move-in Date:  _____ 20_____

## SCREENING DISCLOSURE

1.      DISCLOSURE. The Landlord intends to investigate the information that you have set forth on your application.  This may include obtaining a credit report or other report from a credit bureau or a tenant screening service confirming information that you have set forth in your application.  The Landlord may also contact prior landlords, employers, financial institutions and personal references.

2.      SCREENING FEES. Before the owner will conduct this review of your application, you must pay a tenant-screening fee.  The owner/manager charges a fee of $75.00.  The owner/manager acknowledges receipt of this fee.  This fee represents payment for costs incurred by the landlord to screen your application.  The owner's costs may include costs incurred for a credit report or other screening report, long distance phone calls and for time spent calling landlords, employers, financial institutions, and personal references.

3.      APPLICANT'S RIGHTS. You have a right to dispute the accuracy of the information provided by the tenant screening service, credit bureau, or the entities listed on your application who will be contacted for information about you.  However, the landlord is forbidden by law from giving you certain information about your credit report.  This information may be obtained from the credit bureau or tenant screening agency named below.

4.      TENANT SCREENING SERVICE. The tenant screening service or credit bureau used by the owner, if any is:

_____

5.      COPY RECEIVED. By signing below applicant acknowledges receipt of this notice.


By: _____        _____

[applicant's signature]            [applicant to print name]      [date]


By: _____        _____

[applicant's signature]            [applicant to print name]      [date]

Figure OMP-3

Sample: **Non-Biased Criteria Checklist - Form NCL**

## NONBIAS (MINIMUM RESIDENT STANDARD)

### CRITERIA CHECKLIST

### MINIMUM CRITERIA AND CHECKLIST FOR RESIDENT SELECTION

Automatic disqualification for an apartment

| | |
|---|---|
| | The apartment applied for is in a nonsmoking building, and the applicant(s) smoke. |
| | The building is a non-pet building, and the applicant has a pet(s). |
| | Incomplete application |
| | Applicant lied on application. |
| | Eviction for nonpayment or cause |
| | Case for property damage, disturbances, nuisance, foreclosure, or other cause |
| | Four (4) or more thirty-day delinquencies, three (3) or more sixty-day delinquencies, any combination of four (4) thirty-day or sixty-day delinquencies |
| | One (1) ninety-day or greater delinquency, charge-off, collection, skip, or civil suit |
| | Any repossession, tax lien, or bankruptcy |

Give a score of one point (or more when applicable) for each of the following criteria. Add up the total points to see if the applicant reaches the minimum acceptable score.

| Financial Criteria | |
|---|---|
| | Minimum score on credit report of 650. (Add 1 point for each additional 10 points over 650; deduct 1 point for each 5 points below 650.) |
| | Sufficient income (Monthly income is three times the rent amount.) |
| | Sufficient income (Monthly income is more than four times the rent amount.) |
| | Verifiable source of income of employment |
| | Same source of income for a minimum of one year. (Two years = two points; three years = three points, etc., up to a maximum of five points.) Must provide W-2 forms for proof of income. |
| | Able to pay full deposit and rent requested |
| | Currently paying comparable amount of rent |
| | No negative remarks on credit report |
| | No late payments in past six months on credit report |
| | No excessive financial obligations (more than 50 percent of income) |
| | Has a checking account |
| | Has a savings account |
| | Able to provide three credit references |
| | No late notices from current landlord |
| | No prior evictions |
| | Able to provide a cosigner (two points if cosigner owns real estate) |

\_\_\_\_\_ **Total** (maximum forty points this section).

| Rental Stability Criteria | |
|---|---|
| | Resided at current address minimum of one year. (Two years = two points, three years = three points, etc., up to a maximum of five points.) Must have been responsible for rent payment. |
| | No health or safety violations present upon inspection of current residence |
| | No security deposit to be withheld because of property upkeep at current residence |
| | No notices of any kind from current landlord regarding a rental agreement violation |
| | No neighborhood complaints of residents or pets or police reports on disturbing the peace |
| | No pets |
| | Good report from the landlord prior to the current landlord |
| | No criminal history |
| | |
| | |
| | |

_____ **Total** (maximum fifteen points this section).

| Additional Criteria | |
|---|---|
| | Move-in date within an acceptable time period |
| | Personal appearance and automobile appearance is neat and clean. |
| | Will have rent payments electronically paid month each month (add ten points). |
| | |
| | |
| | |

_____ **Total** (maximum fifteen points this section).

_____ **Total criteria points**

| Applicant's Total Score | | | |
|---|---|---|---|
| Date of application: | | Date verified: | |
| Above criteria verified by: | | Applicant notified | ☐ Acceptance<br>☐ Denial |
| Action taken: | | By what method: | |
| Date applicant notified: | | | |
| Any other action required: | | | |

To be sure that you do not discriminate against any person, please follow the above minimum standard for tenant selection. The applicant who scores highest over the minimum should be selected in order to conform to this nonbiased form.

All applicants who do not score above the minimum criteria can be disqualified. Adverse letter required to comply with Fair Credit Reporting Act.

Figure OMP-4

Sample: **Landlord Verification – Form LLV**

## LANDLORD VERIFICATION

To Whom It May Concern:

<< Applicant Name >>, has recently applied for housing from << *Company* >>.

To assist us in the selection process, please complete the following confidential questions, and fax this form back to us at your earliest convenience.

1. How long was the applicant your tenant?
   _____

2. What was the applicant's monthly rent?
   _____

3. Did the applicant pay his/her rent on time?
   _____

4. Were any complaints from tenants or neighbors ever registered against this applicant?
   _____

5. Did the applicant demonstrate respect for your apartment, its contents, and the surrounding property?
   _____

6. Would you recommend this applicant for tenancy?
   _____

7. How many people occupied this apartment?
   _____

*<< Landlord >>, <<Property Owner >>*     *<< Office Phone >>*

Landlord/Manager Signature _____ Date _____
                          (sign)

Figure OMP-5
_____

Sample: **Prospect Resident Verification – Form TVL**

<< *Date* >>

RE:      << *Applicant Name* >>

To Whom It May Concern:

I hereby authorize you to submit/verify the following information to ABC LLC.  Your prompt attention to this matter will be greatly appreciated.

_____     _____
applicant sign name     applicant print name          applicant sign name     applicant print name

Please complete/verify the following information (*applicable section checked*);

☐      Employment:

From:  _____   To:                       Position:
                                       _____      _____
Salary: $ _____   weekly/monthly/annually:  _____
Comments:
_____

☐   Length of      From:                    20 _____    Rent: $ _____
    Residency     To:                      20 _____
                  Did applicant pay on time?   ☐ Yes    ☐ No
                  Would you rent to this       ☐ Yes    ☐ No
                  individual again?
Comments:

A self-addressed, stamped envelope is provided for your convenience.  If you have any questions, please do not hesitate to call me at << *Office Phone* >>.  Thank you.

Sincerely,


_____
<< *Landlord* >> << *Asset Manager* >>

Figure OMP-6

---

Sample: **Employment Verification – Form EVR**

# EMPLOYMENT VERIFICATION

To Whom It May Concern:

<< *Applicant Name* >>, has recently applied for housing from << *Company* >>. To assist us in the selection process, please complete the following confidential questions, and fax this form back to us at your earliest convenience.

1. Employer's name and address

   _____

2. Length of employment?

   _____

3. Job description?

   _____

4. Is the employee in good standing?

   _____

5. Employee hours?

   _____

6. Employee salary: Weekly $_____ Monthly $_____ Annually $_____

   Commissions _____

Employer's Signature _____ Telephone _____

Employee's authorization to release the above information.

Employee's Signature _____ Date _____

          (sign)

Figure OMP-7

Sample: **Application to Rent – Form ATR**

## APPLICATION TO RENT

SEPARATE APPLICATION REQUIRED FROM EACH APPLICANT UNLESS MARRIED

| THIS SECTION TO BE COMPLETED BY LANDLORD | | |
|---|---|---|
| Address of Property to be Leased: _____ | | |
| Lease Term: Lease From _____ Lease To _____ | | |
| Amounts Due prior to Occupancy: | | |
| First Month's Rent | | $_____ |
| Month(s) Security | | $_____ |
| | Application Fee* | $_____ |
| | Consumer Reports | $_____ |
| | TOTAL: | $_____ |
| *Nonrefundable | | |

| APPLICANT | |
|---|---|
| Full Name: | |
| Current Address: | |
| | Birth Date: |
| | Cell Phone: |
| Home Phone: | Work Phone: |
| Social Security #: | Driver's License Number/State |
| Vehicle Make: | Model: _____ Color: _____ Year: |
| License Plate Number/State: | Smoke: Yes ___ No ___ |
| E-mail Address: | |
| **SPOUSE** | |
| Full Name: | Maiden: |
| Current Address: | |
| | Birth Date: |
| | Cell Phone: |
| Home Phone: | Work Phone: |
| Social Security #: | Driver's License Number/State |
| Vehicle Make: | Model: _____ Color: _____ Year: |
| License Plate Number/State: | Smoke: Yes ___ No ___ |
| E-mail Address: | |

| ADDITIONAL OCCUPANTS: List everyone, including children, who will live with you. | |
|---|---|
| ☐ If this box is checked, there shall be no additional occupant(s). | |
| Full Name | Relationship to Applicant |
| | |
| | |
| | |

Have any of the occupants listed above ever been:

___Convicted of a felony?
Any criminal offense?

| Occupant | Offense | Date Convicted | Time Served |
|---|---|---|---|
| | | | |
| | | | |
| | | | |

___Received deferred adjudication for a felony? ___ Been evicted? ___Broken a lease? ___Declared bankruptcy?

| REFERENCES AND EMERGENCY CONTACTS | |
|---|---|
| Name: | Name: |
| Address: | Address: |
| Telephone: | Telephone: |
| Name: | Name: |
| Address: | Address: |
| Telephone: | Telephone: |

| APPLICANT'S RENTAL HISTORY | |
|---|---|
| Current Address: | |
| Dates Lived at Address: | Reason for Leaving: |
| Landlord/Manager: | Landlord's/Manager's Phone: |
| Previous Address: | |
| Dates Lived at Address: | Reason for Leaving: |
| Landlord/Manager: | Landlord's/Manager's Phone: |

| SPOUSE'S RENTAL HISTORY | |
|---|---|
| Current Address: | |
| Dates Lived at Address: | Reason for Leaving: |
| Landlord/Manager: | Landlord's/Manager's Phone: |
| Previous Address: | |
| Dates Lived at Address: | Reason for Leaving: |
| Landlord/Manager: | Landlord's/Manager's Phone: |

Do you have pets? _____

If so, what kind and breed? _____

Are you looking to have them move in with you? _____

| APPLICANT'S EMPLOYMENT HISTORY | |
|---|---|
| Name and Address of Current Employer: | Phone: |
| Name of Supervisor: | Supervisor's Phone: |
| Employed from: | Position or Title: |
| Name and Address of Previous Employer: | Phone: |
| Name of Supervisor: | Supervisor's Phone: |
| Employed from: | Position or Title: |

| SPOUSE'S EMPLOYMENT HISTORY | |
|---|---|
| Name and Address of Current Employer: | Phone: |
| Name of Supervisor: | Supervisor's Phone: |
| Employed from: | Position or Title: |
| Name and Address of Previous Employer: | Phone: |
| Name of Supervisor: | Supervisor's Phone: |
| Employed from: | Position or Title: |

| APPLICANT'S CREDIT AND FINANCIAL INFORMATION | | | | | |
|---|---|---|---|---|---|
| **Bank/Financial Accounts** | **Bank/Institution** | | **Branch** | | |
| Savings Account: | | | | | |
| Checking Account: | | | | | |
| CD/MM or Similar Account: | | | | | |
| Credit Accounts and Loans | Type of Account (Auto loan, Visa, MC, etc.) | Account Number | Name of Creditor | Amount Owed | Monthly Payment |
| Credit Card | | | | | |
| Credit Card | | | | | |
| Credit Card | | | | | |
| Loans | | | | | |
| Loans | | | | | |
| Loans | | | | | |

| SPOUSE'S CREDIT AND FINANCIAL INFORMATION | | |
|---|---|---|
| **Bank/Financial Accounts** | **Bank/Institution** | **Branch** |
| Savings Account: | | |
| Checking Account: | | |
| CD/MM or Similar Account: | | |

**118**

| Credit Accounts and Loans | Type of Account (Auto loan, Visa, MC, etc.) | Account Number | Name of Creditor | Amount Owed | Monthly Payment |
|---|---|---|---|---|---|
| Credit Card | | | | | |
| Credit Card | | | | | |
| Credit Card | | | | | |
| Loans | | | | | |
| Loans | | | | | |
| Loans | | | | | |

| INCOME | APPLICANT | SPOUSE |
|---|---|---|
| Your gross monthly income (before deductions): | $ | $ |
| Average monthly amounts of other income (specify sources): | $ | $ |
| | | |
| | | |
| TOTAL = | $ | $ |

Thank You!

Thank you for completing an application to rent from us. Please sign below. Please note that a completed application requires submission of the following, which will be attached to this application:

| | | | |
|---|---|---|---|
| _____ | Driver's license | _____ | Two weeks of most current pay stubs for each source listed |
| _____ | Application check | _____ | If self-employed, most current Schedule C tax return and proof of current income |
| | For $ | | |

The above listed applicant(s) declare that all statements made on this application are true and complete. Applicant(s) hereby authorize _____ to verify itself and through its affiliations all of the information in this application and obtain reports on the above-listed applicant and/or applicants. If applicant or applicants have given any false information, _____ is entitled to reject the application and retain all application fees as liquid damages for _____ time and expenses in processing this application.

I recognize that this application for a residence is subject to acceptance or rejection. If application is accepted, lease is to be executed within seven days after applicant is notified of such acceptance. If applicant is not accepted as a resident within three days, the deposit will be returned, except as otherwise noted. If application is accepted and applicant does not sign lease within the above prescribed days after notification, the deposit will be forfeited as liquid damages in payment for holding the apartment off the market.

**Nonrefundable Application**    Date: _____, 20 _____

**Application Fee: $**

By:    _____          _____

        [applicant's signature]              [applicant to print name]


By:    _____          _____

        [applicant's signature]              [applicant to print name]

Figure OMP-8

Sample: **Personal Guarantor – Form PGU**

## PERSONAL GUARANTOR

WHEREAS, _____ "Lessee" has requested that _____ "Landlord" enter into a Contract for the Lease of Real Estate for certain property located in the City of _____, County of _____, State of _____, more commonly known as _____, Apt. _____, _____, _____.

WHEREAS, as an inducement to Landlord to enter into Contract for the Lease of Real Estate, _____ "Guarantor" has agreed to personally guarantee the payment and performance of all of Lessee's obligations, conditions, and covenants as set forth in said Lease Agreement.

NOW, THEREFORE, FOR VALUABLE CONSIDERATION, the receipt and sufficiency of which is hereby acknowledged, Guarantor does hereby unconditionally guarantee that Lessee's obligations, conditions, and covenants will be performed strictly in accordance with the terms of said Lease Agreement regardless of any law, regulation, or order now or hereafter in effect in any jurisdiction affecting the rights of Landlord with respect thereto, to the same extent as if Guarantor under this Guaranty shall be absolute and unconditional irrespective of:

A.      Any lack of validity or enforceability of the Contract for the Lease Agreement;

B.      Any change in the time, manner, or place of payment of, or in any other term of, all or any of the obligations, or any other amendment or waiver of or any consent to departure from the Contract for the Lease Agreement;

C.      Any exchange, release, or non-perfection of any collateral, or any release or amendment or waiver of or consent to departure from any other guaranty, for all or any of the obligations; or

D.      Any other circumstances that might otherwise constitute a defense available to, or a discharge of, the Lessee or any Guarantor.

This Guaranty is a continuing guaranty and shall (i) remain in full force and effect until the fulfillment of all of Lessee's obligations, conditions, and covenants under said Lease Agreement, (ii) be binding upon the Guarantor, its successors and assigns, and (iii) inure to the benefit of and be enforceable by the Landlord and its respective successors, transferees, and assigns. Any liability of the Guarantor shall not be affected by, nor shall it be necessary to procure the consent of the Guarantor or give any notice in reference to, any settlement, or variation of terms of any obligation of the Lessee, or of a Guarantor or any other interested person, by operation of law or otherwise; nor by failure to file, record, or register any security document. Guarantor recognizes that Landlord may utilize various means of attempting to verify Lessee's compliance with the obligations and hereby expressly agrees that such steps are for the sole benefit of Landlord and the adequacy of performance of such checks and examinations shall not be considered as a defense to or mitigation of liability hereunder.

The Guarantor does hereby expressly waive and dispense with notice of acceptance of this Guaranty, notices of nonpayment or nonperformance, notice of amount of indebtedness outstanding at any time, protests, demands, and prosecution of collection, foreclosure, and possessory remedies. The undersigned hereby waives any right to require Landlord to (i) proceed against other persons or Lessee, (ii) advise Guarantor of the results of any checks or examinations, (iii) require Lessee to comply with its agreement with Landlord, or (iv) proceed against Lessee or proceed against or exhaust any security.

Except as noted, Landlord has made no promises to Lessee or Guarantor to induce execution of this Guaranty, and there are no agreements or understandings, either oral or in writing, between the parties affecting this Guaranty. The obligation of all parties signing this guaranty, where more than one, shall be joint and several. No amendment or waiver of any provision of the Guaranty or consent to any departure by the Guarantor therefrom shall in any event be effective unless the same shall be in writing and signed by Landlord.

This Guaranty may not be changed orally and shall bind and inure to the benefit of the heirs, administrators, successors, and assigns of the Lessee and Landlord, respectively. If any part of this Guaranty is not valid or enforceable according to applicable law, all other parts will remain enforceable. This Guaranty and the performance hereunder shall be construed and determined according to the laws of the State of _____.

IN WITNESS WHEREOF THE GUARANTOR HAS EXECUTED THIS GUARANTY this _____day of _____, 20___

_____          _____

(guarantor)                                                    (guarantor)

STATE OF          _____

COUNTY OF          _____

PERSONALLY, came and appeared before me, the undersigned in and for the jurisdiction aforesaid, the within named _____ and _____ in the above and foregoing instrument of writing, who acknowledged to me that they signed and delivered the above foregoing instrument of writing on the day and in the year and for the purposes therein mentioned.

GIVEN under my hand and official seal of office on this the _____ day of _____, 20_____

_____          NOTARY PUBLIC

MY COMMISSION EXPIRES:

_____

Figure OML-1

Sample: **Letter of Acceptance – Form LGA**

*<< Date >>*

*<< Applicant's Name >>*

*<< Applicant's Current Address >>*

*<< City >>, << State >> << Zip >>*

This letter confirms our conversation on [date] at [time], in which you accepted our offer to rent the apartment at [rental property address]. As we discussed, these are the rental terms:

Rent $          Deposit $

Rental start date:        20_____

Rental term: One-year lease, ending on        20_____

Number of occupants: _____

### NO PETS

_____

Deposit and first month's rent total $_____ to be paid by <u>cashier's check</u> or <u>money order</u> on or before

_____ 20_____ at this address: [landlord's address].

Holding deposit of ___[amount]___ to be paid by ___[date]___ at this address _____.

We will sign the rental documents on ___[date]___ at ___[time]___ at ___[address]___.

_____

Thank you for deciding to live here. I look forward to working with you to ensure that your move in and tenancy are smooth and enjoyable. If you have any questions, please don't hesitate to call me.

Yours truly,

_____

*<< Landlord >>, <<Property Owner >>*

Figure OML-2

Sample: **Acceptance Letter with Lease Agreement – Form AGL**

<< *Date* >>

Re:    << *Rental Address* >>

      << *City* >>, << *State* >> << *Zip* >>

Dear << *Mr. Tenant* >> and << *Mrs. Tenant* >>

Thank you for considering making [rental address] your new home. The information that you have provided on your application has been verified, and we would like to take this opportunity to welcome you.

**The Lease Agreement** has been prepared, and we are enclosing it for your review. Please return both copies with your signature so that we can complete the processing of your new apartment home.

Remember that time is of the essence with your paperwork.

Sincerely,

_____

<< *Landlord* >>, <<*Property Owner* >>

**(Note: This letter and the Lease Agreement should be sent out certified mail, return-receipt requested.)**

Figure OML-3

## Sample: **Month-to-Month Pet Agreement – Form MPA**

### Month-to-Month Pet Agreement

Pet owners must complete a **Pet Application and Registration Form**. If the pet is either a dog or a cat, a current photograph **MUST** be attached.

This Pet Agreement dated << *Date* >> is attached to and forms a part of the "Month-to-Month Tenant Lease Agreement" dated _____, 20___, between << *Landlord* >> and << *Mr. Tenant* >> and << *Mrs. Tenant* >> Tenant, for the residential unit located at << *Rental Address* >> << *City* >>, << *State* >> << *Zip* >>.

Tenant Home Telephone: _____ Tenant Work Telephone: _____

| PET'S NAME | TYPE/BREED | AGE | LICENSE NUMBER |
|---|---|---|---|
|  |  |  |  |
|  |  |  |  |

Tenant desires to keep pet(s) in the dwelling Tenant occupies under the Lease Agreement referred to above, and because the new landlord does not permit pets, this agreement was drawn, allowing the tenant to keep the pet until the termination of the lease in force at the signing of this agreement. Tenant to pay an additional rent in the amount of $25 per pet under this tenancy. Tenant to provide copy of vaccinations and certificates of health for each pet.

Tenant Agrees to:

1) Keep the pet under control at all times.
2) Keep the pet restrained, but not tethered, when it is outside the apartment.
3) Not leave the pet unattended for any unreasonable periods.
4) Dispose of the pet's droppings properly and quickly.
5) Not leave food or water for the pet or any other animal outside the dwelling.
6) Pay immediately for any damage, loss, or expense caused by the pet and in addition, tenant will add $300 to Tenant's security, any of which may be used for cleaning, repairs, or delinquent rent when Tenant vacates. This added deposit, or what remains of it when pet damages have been assessed, will be returned to Tenant within thirty days after Tenant proves this or any pets are no longer on the premises.
7) The Landlord reserves the right to revoke permission to keep the pet should Tenant break this agreement.
8) Tenant agrees to have the Premises exterminated for ticks and fleas upon vacating and shall furnish Landlord a copy of the exterminator's receipt.

By: _____
(Tenant) (Date)

By: _____
(Tenant) (Date)

By: _____
Landlord (Property Owner) (Date)

Figure OML-4

Sample: **Pet Agreement – Form PAC**

## Pet Agreement

### (BECOMES A PART OF LEASE CONTRACT)

> Note: Pets are a serious responsibility and risk for each Resident in the building. If not properly controlled and cared for, pets can disturb the rights of others and cause damages running into many hundreds of dollars, for which the Resident may be held liable.

This Pet Agreement is entered into this ____day of _____, _____. All deposits required will be paid prior to occupancy. In consideration of their mutual promises, Management and Residents agree as follows:

**1.** **Dwelling Unit Description**

Apt. No. _____ Street Address: _____ City: _____ State: __

Lease Description:

Date of Lease _____

Residents (List all residents)

_____        _____

_____        _____

_____        _____

Such lease will be referred to in this Pet Agreement as the "Lease."

**2.** **Conditional Authorization for Pet**

The lease covering the Premises provides that no pets are permitted on or about the Premises without Management's prior written consent. Any pet may be rejected by the Management for any reason Management deems appropriate. Management reserves the right to deny an Application for Permission to have a Pet or Pet Agreement due to an animal, breed, or animal mixed with a breed with a history of aggressive behavior. Residents are hereby authorized to keep a pet, which is described below, on the Premises of the above dwelling unit until the above-described Lease expires. Authorization may be terminated sooner if Residents' right of occupancy is lawfully terminated or if the pet rules listed below are violated in any way by Residents or Residents' guests or occupants.

**3.** **Additional Security Deposit**

The total security deposit as required in the Lease shall be increased by **$400** (less $125 at move out). Such additional deposit shall be considered as a general security deposit for any and all purposes. Refund of the security deposit shall be subject to all terms and conditions set forth in the Lease. The additional security deposit is not refundable prior to surrender of the premises by all

**126**

Residents, even if pet has been removed. The pet security deposit may not be processed by Owner for up to forty-five (45) days after Residents have vacated the apartment. This time allows for any evidence of flea infestation and resurfacing of pet stains and odors that may not be readily apparent immediately after steam cleaning.

## 4. Additional Monthly Rent

The total monthly rent as stated in the Lease shall be increased by $75. Additional monthly rent will be effective this _____ day of _____, _____.

## 5. No Limit Liability

The additional monthly rent and additional security deposit under this Pet Agreement is not a limit on Residents' liability for property damages, cleaning, deodorization, defleaing, replacements, and/or personal injuries as set forth in this agreement.

A. Cleaning and Repairs: **Residents shall be jointly and severally liable for the entire amount of all damages caused by the Pet. If any item cannot be satisfactorily cleaned or repaired, Residents must pay for complete replacement of such item. Pet odors and stains are "extraordinary damage" and NOT "normal wear and tear."**

B. Injuries: Residents shall be strictly liable for the entire amount of any injury to any person or property caused by the pet and shall indemnify Management for all cost of litigation and attorney's fees resulting from same.

## 6. Description of Pet

Only the following described pet is authorized to be kept in Residents' dwelling unit. **No substitutions are allowed.** No other pet (including offspring) shall be permitted on the premises by Residents' guests or occupants at any time. **No visiting pets.** This prohibition includes birds (except those that are caged), bullmastiffs, bull terriers, chinchillas, chow chows, Doberman pinschers, ferrets, fish (in tanks twenty gallons or more without adequate insurance naming the Management as additional insured), German shepherds, iguanas, insects, malamutes, monkeys, pit bulls (a.k.a. American Staffordshire terriers, Staffordshire bull terriers, or American pit bull terriers), pot-bellied pigs, rabbits, raccoons, Rhodesian Ridgebacks, rodents of any kind, Rottweilers, Siberian Huskies, skunks, snakes or reptiles of any kind, tarantulas, scorpions, or spiders of any kind, and weasels. See SPECIFICALLY PROHIBITED BREEDS (below).

## 7. Housebroken

Pets must be housebroken! Name of pet: _____.

Type: _____

Breed: _____

Age: _____ Weight: _____ full grown.

License Number: _____ (copy required).

Date of last rabies shot: _____ (copy required).

Veterinarian: _____

Name of Pet Owner: _____

## 8. The MAXIMUM Weight of Any Pet May Not Exceed Forty (40) Pounds.

9. **Specifically Prohibited Breeds: The Following Specific Breeds of Dogs (or Dogs Mixed with These Breeds) Are Not Permitted:**

Bullmastiffs, bull terriers, chow chows, Doberman pinschers, German shepherds, malamutes, pit bulls (a.k.a. American Staffordshire terriers, Staffordshire bull terriers, or American pit bull terriers), Rhodesian Ridgebacks, and Siberian Huskies. Dogs must be contained in an area (cage) so as not to interfere with any maintenance service that has been requested. No wild animals are permitted such as birds (except those that are caged), chinchillas, ferrets, fish (in tanks twenty gallons or more without adequate insurance naming Management as additional insured), iguanas, monkeys, pot-bellied pigs, rabbits, raccoons, rodents of any kind, skunks, snakes or reptiles of any kind, tarantulas, scorpions, or spiders of any kind, and weasels.

10. **Specific Types of Pets**

The following rules apply to specific types of pets:

DOGS: Must be spayed or neutered. Veterinary proof is required. No puppies (four [4] months or less) are allowed. No adult dog, fully grown, will exceed forty (40) pounds.

CATS: No cat is permitted unless it has been declawed and spayed or neutered. Veterinary proof is required. Your cat must be kept in the apartment at all times except when transporting the cat. Under no circumstances are cats allowed on apartment balconies or in common indoor or outdoor areas. Cat litter must be double-bagged in plastic prior to disposal in the garbage. Use of a litter box is required, and regular disposal of waste and cleaning is required. You may not dispose of litter in toilets, even if the litter is marked "flushable." Cat litter can cause clogs in the pipes and flooding. Residents shall be responsible for all damage caused by violations of these rules.

FISH: Stand must be sturdy. No aquarium with a capacity greater than twenty (20) gallons shall be kept on the Premises or in any apartment. Residents must place aquariums in a safe location in the apartment, on a shelf or table giving the aquarium enough support. Residents shall be responsible for all damage caused by leakage or breakage from any aquarium. Residents shall provide proof of adequate insurance naming Management as additionally insured if aquarium is twenty (20) gallons or more.

11. **Severability**

If any clause or provision of this Pet Agreement is illegal, invalid, or unenforceable under present or future laws effective during the term, then it is the intention of the parties hereto that the remainder of this Pet Agreement shall not be affected thereby. It is also the intention of the parties to this Pet Agreement that in lieu of each clause or provision that is illegal, invalid, or unenforceable, there shall be added as a part of this Pet Agreement a clause or provision as similar in terms or effect to such legal, invalid, or unenforceable clause or provision as may be possible, valid, and enforceable.

12. **Pet Rules**

Residents are responsible for the actions of the pet at all times. Residents agree to abide by the following rules:

A. Nuisance: Residents agree that a pet will not disturb the rights, comforts, and conveniences of neighbors or other Residents. This applies whether the pet is inside or outside of Residents' dwelling. Pet may not cause damage to the property.

B. Sanitary Problems: Dogs, cats, and guide animals for handicapped persons must be HOUSEBROKEN. All other pets must be caged when owners are not present. The pet may not be allowed to urinate or defecate on any unprotected carpet, vinyl floor, or hardwood floor inside the dwelling. Residents shall not permit the pet to defecate or urinate anywhere on the property, including dwelling units, patio areas, walkways, stairs, stairwells, parking lots, grassy areas, or other places. Residents must take the pet off the property for that purpose. If pet defecation is permitted inside the dwelling unit or on patio areas, it shall be done in litter boxes with "kitty litter" type mix. If pet defecation occurs anywhere on the property (including fenced yards for Residents' exclusive use), Residents shall be responsible for the immediate removal of waste in the dwelling or on the grounds and repair of any damage. There will be a seventy-five-dollar ($75) charge assessed for each occurrence of Management cleanup of pet waste.

C. Residents will have sanitary waste removers, commonly called a "Pooper-Scooper" or "Pet Scooper," at all times while walking the pet outside the unit and agree to remove and properly dispose of any pet waste.

D. Pets shall not be tied to any fixed object outside the dwelling unit, including patio areas, walkways, stairs, stairwells, parking lots, grassy areas, or any other part of the property. This does not apply in fenced yards (if any) that are for Residents' exclusive use.

E. Prohibited Areas: Residents shall not permit pets in laundry room, storage areas, and other dwelling units.

F. Feeding of Pets: Residents' pet must be fed and watered inside the dwelling unit; pet food or water may not be left outside the dwelling unit at any time. This does not apply in fenced yards (if any) that are for Residents' exclusive use.

G. Supervision: Pets shall be kept on a leash and under Residents' supervision when outside the dwelling or Residents' private fenced yard area. Owner shall have the right to pick up unleashed pets and/or report them to the proper authorities. Owner shall impose reasonable charges for picking up and/or keeping unleashed pets. Residents agree to comply with all applicable governmental laws and regulations (Leash Laws).

## 13. Additional Rules

Management shall from time to time have the right to make reasonable changes and additions to the above pet rules, if in writing, and distribute to all Residents who are permitted to have pets.

## 14. Violation of Rules

If any rules or provisions of this Pet Agreement is violated by Residents or Residents' guests or occupants in the sole judgment of Management, Residents shall immediately (within forty-eight [48] hours) and permanently remove the pet from the premises upon written notice from Management; and Management shall have all other rights and remedies set forth in the Lease, including damages, eviction, and/or attorney's fees.

## 15. Complaints About Pet

Residents agree to immediately and permanently remove the pet from the premises if Management receives reasonable complaints from neighbors or other Residents or if Management, in Management's sole discretion, determines that the pet has disturbed the rights, comforts, or conveniences of neighbors or other Residents.

## 16. Removal of Pet by Management

If, in Management's reasonable judgment, Residents have (1) abandoned the pet, (2) left the pet in the dwelling unit for an extended period of time without food or water, (3) failed to care for a sick pet, (4) violated Management's pet rules, or (5) repeatedly allowed the pet to defecate or urinate in places other than designated areas designated by Management, Management may, after giving written notice, enter the dwelling unit with the proper authorities and remove the pet. Management may turn the pet over to a Humane Society or local authority. Management has no lien on the pet for any purpose, but Residents shall pay for reasonable care and kenneling charges for such pet. Any animal that causes or appears to be a threat to any person on the leased premises or any animal, breed, or animal mixed with a breed with a history of aggressive behavior will be considered a dangerous animal, and Management retains the right to remove it immediately!

### 17. Liability for Damages, Cleaning, Etc.

Residents shall be jointly and severally liable for the entire amount of all damages caused by such pet and all cleaning, defleaing, and deodorizing required because of such pet. This applies to carpets, doors, walls, drapes, wallpaper, window, screens, furniture, appliances, and any other part of the dwelling unit, landscaping, or other improvement on the property. If such items cannot be satisfactorily cleaned or repaired, Residents must be pay for complete replacement by Management. Payment for damages, repairs, cleanings, replacements, etc. shall be due immediately upon demand. **Residents shall be strictly liable for the entire amount of injury to the person or property of others, caused by such pet; Residents shall indemnify Management for all cost of litigation and attorney's fees resulting from same.**

### PET DAMAGE OF ANY KIND IS NOT CONSIDERED

### NORMAL WEAR AND TEAR

### 18. Move Out

Upon move out, Residents shall pay for defleaing, deodorizing, and/or steam cleaning to protect future Residents from possible health hazards, regardless of how long the pet occupied the premises. Such steam cleaning, defleaing, and/or deodorization may be arranged by Management. An amount of seventy-five dollars ($75) will be withheld from the Pet Deposit for this purpose.

### 19. Multiple Residents

Each Resident who signed the Lease shall sign this Pet Agreement. Residents and Residents' guests or occupants shall abide by all pet rules. Each Resident shall be jointly and severally liable for damages and all other obligations set forth herein, even if such Resident does not own the pet.

### 20. General

Residents acknowledge that no other oral or written agreement exists regarding this Pet Agreement. Except for written rule changes pursuant to paragraph 12 hereof, Management has no authority to modify this Pet Agreement or the pet rules unless in writing. This Pet Agreement and the Pet Rules shall be considered as part of the Lease Contract described above. It has been executed in multiple copies, one for Residents and one or more for Management.

Written notice regarding pet(s) to any one party on the Lease shall constitute notice to all parties on the Lease.

### THIS IS A BINDING LEGAL DOCUMENT—READ CAREFULLY BEFORE SIGNING

Resident or Residents
(All Residents must sign)

Management or Owner

_____

(Signature)          (Date)

_____

(Signature)          (Date)

_____

(Signature)          (Date)

Figure OML-5

Sample: **Tenant Move-in Checklist – Form TMB**

# Tenant Move-In Checklist

| << Property >> | << Mr. Tenant >> |
|---|---|

| Agent: | << Move-In-Date >> |
|---|---|

|  |  | By | Date |
|---|---|---|---|
| 1. | Completed application received. | _____ | _____ |
| a. | Copy of Driver's License | _____ | _____ |
| b. | Copy of Pay Stubs | _____ | _____ |
| c. | Verification Approval | _____ | _____ |
| 2. | Application and credit fees received and recorded. | _____ | _____ |
| 3. | Unit assigned, posted to Vacancy Report. | _____ | _____ |
| 4. | Deposit received and recorded. | _____ | _____ |
| 5. | Unit inspected and work assigned. | _____ | _____ |
| 6. | Credit check completed. | _____ | _____ |
| 7. | Applicant notified of approval/rejection. | _____ | _____ |

**(If Prospect is Rejected, Checklist Ends Here)**

| 8. | Appointment for signing lease: | _____ | _____ |
|---|---|---|---|
|  | Date: _____ Time: _____ | _____ | _____ |
| 9. | Move-In date scheduled: | _____ | _____ |
|  | Date: _____ Time: _____ | _____ | _____ |
| 10 | Utilities transferred or turned off/on. | _____ | _____ |
| 11 | Keys readied. | _____ | _____ |
| 12 | Final unit inspection made. | _____ | _____ |
| 13 | Signed Certificate of Occupancy. | _____ | _____ |

14    Rent, security deposit and other monies received.          \_\_\_\_\_    _____

15    Welcome package/orientation information readied.          \_\_\_\_\_    _____

16    Other          \_\_\_\_\_    _____

17    Closing          \_\_\_\_\_    _____

  a.    Condominium / Single Family Lease Agreement          \_\_\_\_\_    _____

  b.    Option to Purchase Addendum          \_\_\_\_\_    _____

  c.    Rules and Policies for Tenants          \_\_\_\_\_    _____

  d.    Approval of Rental / RTO Application          \_\_\_\_\_    _____

  e.    Disclosure / RTO Disclosure          \_\_\_\_\_    _____

  f.    Receipt for Keys          \_\_\_\_\_    _____

  g.    Authorization for Automatic Collection of Rent/Late Fee          \_\_\_\_\_    _____

  h.    NAIL Authorization          \_\_\_\_\_    _____

  i.    Central Station Life Safety System          \_\_\_\_\_    _____

  j.    Renters' Insurance          \_\_\_\_\_    _____

  k.    Tenant Lead Paint Warning          \_\_\_\_\_    _____

18    Walk-through with resident completed.          \_\_\_\_\_    _____

19    Move-in inspection completed, signed by resident.          \_\_\_\_\_    _____

20    Move-in completed.          \_\_\_\_\_    _____

21    Resident files set-up.          \_\_\_\_\_    _____

Figure OML-6

Sample: **Document Receipt Acknowledgement – Form DRA**

## DOCUMENT RECEIPT ACKNOWLEDGEMENT FORM

I/we, the undersigned Tenant(s), have received copies of the following forms from

_____(Lessor/Landlord)

Tenants: Please place your initials next to each of the documents noted below that you have received and then date and sign the bottom of this page.

| INITIAL | INITIAL | |
|---------|---------|---|
| ☐ _____ | _____ | Lease or Rental Agreement |
| ☐ _____ | _____ | House Rules and Policies |
| ☐ _____ | _____ | Lead-Based Paint Disclosure Statement |
| ☐ | | EPA *Protect Your Family From Lead In Your Home* booklet |
| ☐ _____ | _____ | Mold/Mildew Addendum |
| ☐ _____ | _____ | Smoke Detector Acknowledgement Form |
| ☐ _____ | _____ | Renter's Insurance |
| ☐ _____ | _____ | List of Special Provisions and Addendum |
| ☐ _____ | _____ | Tenant Move-In Checklist* |
| ☐ _____ | _____ | Inventory Checklist* |
| ☐ _____ | _____ | Damage Charges |

*The tenant must return a copy of the completed checklist to the Lessor within seven days from the date shown below.

Date: _____        _____
                               Tenant's Signature

Date: _____        _____
                               Tenant's Signature

Figure OML-7

Sample: **Welcome New Resident – Form WNR**

### Welcome New Resident

We hope that you will enjoy your new home. To assist you in being settled, we would like to take this opportunity to explain some of our services and the property's policies, procedures, and rules.

### LANDLORD

| The Landlord maintains the following schedule: | Monday | through | 10:00 a.m. | to | 4:00 p.m. |
|---|---|---|---|---|---|
| | Friday | | | | |
| | Saturday | | 10:00 a.m. | to | 2:00 p.m. |
| | Sunday | | Closed | | Closed |

If you have any problem or need any information about your residence, please feel free to call us at: << *Office Phone* >>

### PAYMENT OF RENT

Rents are due in full on the first day of the month.

Mail checks to: << *Mail Checks To* >>

<< *Company Address* >>

Your rent becomes delinquent on the tenth day of the month. Payments not received by the tenth of the month are subject to a $50 late charge (and an additional $1 for each subsequent day until the delinquent rent is paid.) You may also make a cash payment to the landlord to stop additional penalties.

### MAINTENANCE

You are responsible for the routine upkeep of your residence. You are responsible to make all necessary repairs costing less than $150. To request service, please contact the Resident Manager during normal working hours. If an emergency occurs when the office is closed, please call: (XXX) XXX-XXXX.

Management is responsible for maintenance and repairs necessitated by normal wear and usage. Repair of damage caused by resident negligence or misuse is the responsibility of the resident. In such cases, the maintenance staff will make the repairs, but the resident will be charged for the cost of labor and materials.

Figure OML-8

Sample: **House Rules and Policies**

House Rules and Policies

---

**Welcome to Your New Home!**

Every effort will be made to provide you with a pleasant atmosphere in which to reside. To achieve this and ensure health, welfare, and safety, we ask all tenants to cooperate with the following House Rules and Policies, which are part of the Lease Agreement.

**Your apartment is your home and should be treated in that respect.**

**Please respect the property of others.**

Repeated violations of these **House Rules and Policies** that disrupt the livability of the apartment community, adversely affect the health or safety of any person or the right of any Tenant to the quiet enjoyment of the leased premises, or have any adverse effect on the management of the apartment community, will be deemed grounds for termination of the **Lease Agreement.**

House Rules and Policies

**Section One**

I.  **GENERAL**
    - This agreement is an addendum and part of the **Lease Agreement** between **Landlord** and **Tenant**.
    - New rules and policies or amendments to these rules may be adopted upon giving thirty (30) days' notice in writing. These rules and any changes or amendments have a legitimate purpose and are not intended to be arbitrary or work as a substantial modification of Tenant rights. They will not be unequally enforced. Tenant is responsible for the conduct of guests and the adherence to these rules and regulations at all times.
    - Tenant cannot use the premises for anything unlawful or in such manner as to interfere unreasonably with the use by another occupant.
    - Tenant shall not make any apartment-to-apartment canvass to solicit business or information, or to distribute any article or material to or from other tenants or occupants of the community, and shall not exhibit, sell, or offer to sell, use, rent, or exchange any products of services in or from the apartment.
    - When the Tenant has a new telephone number, he or she must communicate this information to the Landlord.

## A. NOISE AND CONDUCT

- Tenants shall not make or allow any disturbing noises in the apartment by tenant, family, or guests nor permit anything by such persons that will interfere with the rights, comforts, or conveniences of other persons.
- All musical instruments, television sets, stereos, radios, etc., are to be played at a volume that will not disturb other persons.
- The activities and conduct of tenant, tenant's guests, and minor children of tenant or guests, outside of the apartment on the common grounds and parking areas, must be reasonable at all times and not annoy or disturb other persons.
- No lounging, visiting, or loud talking that may be disturbing to other tenants will be allowed in the common areas at any time.
- No clothing, curtains, or other items shall be hung from balconies or out of windows.

## B. CLEANLINESS AND TRASH

- The apartment must be kept clean, sanitary, and free from objectionable odors.
- Tenant shall assist management in keeping the outside common areas clean.
- No littering of papers, cigarette butts, or trash is allowed.
- No trash or other materials may be accumulated that will cause a hazard or be in violation of any health, fire, or safety ordinance or regulation.
- Garbage is to be placed inside the containers provided, and lids should not be slammed. Garbage should not be allowed to accumulate and should be placed in the outside containers on a daily basis.
- Furniture must be kept inside the apartment. All personal belongings must be kept inside or in storage areas approved in writing by Management. Any items outside the apartment, unless approved in writing, are subject to removal by Management. Tenant may be charged for the cost of removal.
- Articles are not to be left in the hallways or other common areas.
- Clothing, curtains, rugs, etc. shall not be shaken or hung outside of any ledge or balcony.

## C. SAFETY

- No smoking is allowed in the common areas of the property.
- All doors must be locked during the absence of tenant.
- All appliances except refrigerators must be turned off before leaving the apartment.
- When leaving for more than five (5) days, Tenant shall notify management how long Tenant will be away.
- The use or storage of gasoline, cleaning solvent, or other combustibles in the apartment is prohibited.
- No personal belongings, including bicycles, play equipment, or other items, may be placed in the halls, stairways, or about the building.
- Children on the premises must be supervised by a responsible adult at all times.
- Candles may not be burned in bedrooms.

## D. MAINTENANCE, REPAIRS, AND ALTERATIONS

- It shall be the responsibility of Tenant to regularly test the smoke and carbon monoxide detector(s) to ensure that the devices are in operable condition. Tenant will inform Management immediately, in writing, of any defect, malfunction, or failure of such detectors. Tenant is responsible for replacing batteries, if any, as needed unless otherwise prohibited by law.

- Tenant shall advise Management in writing of any items requiring repair (dripping faucets, faulty light switches, etc.). Notification should be immediate in an emergency, or for normal problems, within business hours. Repair request should be made as soon as the defect is noted.
- Service request should not be made to maintenance people or other such personnel.
- Costs of repair or clearance of stoppages in waste pipes or drains, water pipes, or plumbing fixtures caused by Tenant's negligence or improper usage are the responsibility of Tenant. Payment for corrective action must be paid by Tenant on demand.
- No alterations or improvements shall be made by Tenant without the consent of management. Any article attached to the woodwork, walls, floors, or ceilings shall be the sole responsibility of Tenant. Tenant shall be liable for any repairs necessary during or after residency to restore premises to the original condition.

# House Rules and Policies

### Section Two

The following are general rules that you will be expected to follow:

ADVERTISEMENTS: Tenant shall not allow any sign, advertisement, or notice to be placed inside or outside the building. There will be **no** rummage or furniture sales. No signs, stickers, or notes are to be posted on the apartment entry door or windows.

ALCOHOL CONSUMPTION: Alcohol consumption is only allowed in the apartment or on your personal patio/porch area. Consumption of alcohol in any public/common area is not permitted.

ANTENNAS/DISHES: Tenant is not allowed to install a video antenna device or DBS satellite dish, hereinafter collectively referred to as a "dish."

APPLIANCES: The installation of a full-sized dishwasher, washing machine, and dryer is prohibited. Air conditioners (manufactured for the in-wall sleeves) are permitted with prior management approval.

BALCONIES AND PATIOS: All balconies and patios must be kept clean and neat. This includes but is not limited to no furnishings unless they are specifically designed for outdoor or lawn use, no beer kegs, no trash bins or cans, no storage of potentially dangerous, flammable, poisonous, or hazardous materials.

BANNED INDIVIDUALS FROM THE PROPERTY: Management reserves the right to ban any individual from the property and/or entering the building. Tenants are strictly forbidden to allow these individuals on the property or into the building. Tenants who allow banned individuals on to the property, into the building, or into their units may be subject to eviction action as allowed by state law.

CARPETING: The carpet installed in your apartment is flame resistant, as required by law. However, if a hot ash is dropped on it, a burn hole will occur. Burn holes or other damage to your carpet will be charged to the tenant. Please advise Management as soon as possible if any such incident should occur, so that it may be corrected.

CARPET CLEANING DURING TENANCY: It is Tenant's responsibility to keep the carpeting clean. Therefore, management recommends that Tenant have the carpeting professionally cleaned during his or her tenancy to avoid additional charges. **An excessively dirty carpet is not considered normal wear and tear and is therefore subjected to an additional cleaning or replacement cost at move out.**

CARPET CLEANING AT MOVE-OUT: Tenant must have the carpet professionally cleaned at move out. A receipt must be presented by the last day of occupancy, or the tenant will be charged $100 per carpeted room for the cleaning. If the carpet is unable to be cleaned or needs to be replaced due to conditions made by the tenant, the tenant will be charged for the replacement of same, minus wear and tear.

CHARCOAL AND GAS GRILLS: Charcoal and gas grills are never to be used for any purpose within the apartment or on the patio or balcony of the apartment.

CEILINGS AND FLOORS: Tenants and their guests shall not damage or disturb any part of the ceiling or floor in the apartment in any way, including but not limited to: installing hooks, nails, or other hardware in the ceiling; drilling in the ceiling; hanging plants, light fixtures, or other objects from the ceiling; allowing water to accumulate on the floor; and/or painting, repairing, or making improvements with respect to the ceiling or floor. Tenant shall immediately report any sagging, warping, leaking, cracking, staining, holes, or water accumulation related to the ceiling or floor to Management. **Any damage the tenant causes to the ceiling or floor, including but not limited to damage caused by tenant's violation of the above shall not constitute ordinary wear and tear. The tenant shall be responsible for reimbursing Management for the cost of repairing damage to the ceiling or floor and for any damages that result as the consequence of the tenant's action.**

CHRISTMAS TREE DISPOSAL: Once the holidays are over, please dispose of your tree as directed by Management.

CRIMINAL ACTIVITY: Criminal and drug activity committed by any member of the household, whether on or off the property, is prohibited. Criminal and sex offender background checks will be run before the annual lease renewal process. Anyone who may be a threat to the health, safety, and welfare of other residents in the community will not have his or her lease renewed. Fair Housing laws do not protect criminal activity.

- Having a criminal record is not a protected class under fair housing laws.
- A **conviction** means that a judge and jury have determined that the individual is guilty of a particular crime. An **arrest** occurs if law enforcement suspects the individual committed a crime.
- **Adjudication withheld** means the court determined the individual did the crime, but the court is not entering a conviction at the moment. Instead, the court places certain conditions on the defendant (i.e., do community service; do not do drugs).

DAMAGE TO THE APARTMENT/COMMON AREAS: Tenants will be strictly held responsible for damages in their apartments and to the common areas. The tenant is also responsible for any damage done by his or her guests. A written bill will be sent shortly after the damage is noticed, and payment is expected promptly upon receipt. Further maintenance that is required beyond usual wear and tear will be charged to the tenant(s).

DELIVERIES/SOLICITATION: Management will not accept any deliveries for any tenants. No solicitation of any kind is permitted in the building or on the grounds.

DISTURBANCES: The tenant agrees not to permit noises, loud voices, acts, or odors that will disturb the rights or comfort of neighbors. The tenant agrees to keep the volume of any radio, CD player, stereo, television, or musical instrument at a level that will not disturb the neighbors. Tenants agree not to let their guests, visitors, or children disturb their neighbors as well.

ENTRANCES: No outside doors are to be propped open under any circumstances to allow tenants or visitors entry without the use of a key or the intercom system.

FIREARM: Possession of firearms on the premises is **not** allowed under any circumstances.

FIRE EXTINGUISHERS: Every apartment is equipped with a five-pound ABC dry-chemical fire extinguisher.

FIRE EXTINGUISHER INSPECTIONS: In compliance with state and local fire codes, the fire extinguisher in your apartment must be inspected by a qualified outside agency once a year. This inspection requires entry into each apartment by inspection company personnel, accompanied by management. You will be given at least thirty days' notification.

FIREWORKS: Storing or using fireworks on the premises is strictly forbidden. This includes but is not limited to sparklers, Roman candles, bottle rockets, smoke bombs, firecrackers, etc.

GAMES: Skateboarding and games such as darts, baseball, softball, and stickball are not permitted on the property. Archery sets, BB guns, and anything that fires a projectile are considered dangerous weapons and are **not allowed** on the property.

GARBAGE/RECYCLING: Tenant will not allow garbage, newspapers, or other refuse to remain in the apartment to litter the halls or the outside of the building. All garbage must be wrapped, tied, and deposited in the receptacles provided by Management.

GARAGE/CARPORT: Landlord grants permission to **tenants** to occupy the garage indicated in the Rent Summary on Page One (1) of this Lease Agreement. Tenant is subject to the following terms:

- Tenant acknowledges that the garage/carport is for parking of vehicles only. Tenant acknowledges that the garages is not air conditioned and that storing of personal items in the garage is strictly prohibited. Therefore, Landlord assumes no responsibility for personal belongings stored within the garage. Tenant shall not keep any pets in the garage nor store any explosives, fireworks, or any other item or substance that Landlord deems dangerous.
- No electricity may be hooked up to the garage or carport, and no plants may be grown within the garage or storage unit.
- Tenant further understands that the Landlord does not provide security services for Tenant or any of Tenant's belongings in the garage or carport. Landlord will not be liable for any damages, loss, or injury to persons or property occurring within or about the garage or carport, whether caused by the Landlord, someone else, weather, fire, rain, flood, or any other act of God.
- Tenant is responsible for the electronic door opener. The deposit, if placed, will be refunded if door opener is returned upon move-out and is in operable condition.
- Tenant is responsible for the maintenance and care of the fixtures inside the garage and may not remove them for any reason.
- Tenant is responsible for all damages and agrees to reimburse Landlord for all such damages.
- The garage door shall be closed at all times with the exception of entering or exiting the garage.
- Landlord reserves the right of entry into garage for inspection, repair, alteration, or other reasonable business purpose connected with the operation of the property.

GASOLINE-POWERED EQUIPMENT: Gasoline, kerosene, solvents, and other flammable liquids are not to be stored in the building, apartment, hallways, or in storage areas.

GUESTS/VISITORS: Tenant shall be responsible for guests/visitors at all times. Guests/visitors are not allowed to loiter or play in the halls, stairways, elevators, lawns, or other areas used by the public and other tenants. Any person who stays longer than fourteen days in a twelve-month period will be considered a tenant and in violation of the Lease Agreement provisions regarding household composition.

INSURANCE: The tenant must obtain his or her own personal renter's insurance. The Owner and Management are not responsible for theft or for the damage to personal property from any source in the apartments, laundry room, storage area, or any other portions of the premises. A copy of the policy must be given to Landlord.

KEYS: Each tenant will receive two (2) apartment door keys, two (2) apartment dead bolt keys, two (2) vestibule door keys, and one (1) mailbox key. If the keys are lost or stolen, there will be a replacement charge to the tenant: apartment door key: $10.00; apartment dead bolt key: $15.50; vestibule door key: $7.00; mailbox key: $15.00; key fobs: $50.00 when used. Chain locks are not permitted.

LAUNDRY ROOM: Washers and dryers are for the use of the tenants. The washing and drying of laundry by outsiders is prohibited. Each tenant is responsible for leaving the laundry room in a neat and orderly fashion and for following all instructions for equipment use. Note: Lint must be removed from the dryer with each use, for efficiency and fire safety. Lint should be placed in the appropriate garbage containers. No one is allowed to leave his or her laundry in the washer or dryer for thirty minutes after completion without it being removed to a basket or to a folding table to allow someone else the use the washer and/or dryer. If a machine is not functioning properly, place the out-of-order sign on it and call the appropriate service number. Management will not be liable for any loss, damage, or injury to persons or property from whatever cause as a result of Tenant's use of the laundry equipment.

LIGHTS: The tenant is responsible for the replacement of lightbulbs within his or her apartment.

LIVE-IN AIDE: There are times that a tenant may require a **live-in aide** to live with him or her due to a disability. If the tenant requests that the aide not be on the lease or on the income-certification paperwork, this situation will be determined by the following assessment:

- Is there enough physical room to house the aide?
- Will having the aide impose an undue hardship, including an unreasonable financial burden?
- Will the aide hold up to a background check?

LOCKS: Tenant shall not attach or permit to be attached additional locks or similar devices to any door or window, change existing locks or the mechanism thereof, or make or permit to be made any keys for any door other than those provided by Management. Tenant, upon termination of tenancy, shall deliver to the manager all keys that have been furnished Tenant or that Tenant has made, and in the event of loss of any keys, to pay Management for replacement.

LOITERING: Loitering is not permitted on the lawns, sidewalks, entries, halls, stairways, or parking areas.

MOVE-OUT PRIOR TO THE EXPIRATION OF LEASE: Each tenant must realize that moving out prior to the expiration of the lease does not release either the individual or other tenants (and guarantors if applicable) on the lease. All tenants are jointly and severally liable for the full performance of all lease obligations. This means you are each responsible for your roommates. Management does not differentiate between you individually; with respect to this, you are all treated as a group. If you move out prior to the expiration of the lease, you must notify Management in writing and return your keys. You will remain responsible for payment of rent and other charges until the earlier of the original expiration of your lease or our leasing the apartment to new tenants who actually take possession. In addition, you may be held responsible for leasing costs that may include but not be limited to cleaning the apartment, painting, advertising, etc. If you move out and fail to pay rent, Management may go to court and obtain a judgment for monetary damages against all or one of the tenants and one or all of the guarantors of the lease. If an individual moves out of the apartment and the others remain, all those on the lease will continue to be bound by the terms of the lease. However, should you want to assign part of the lease to a new individual, you must come to the office and have a release signed by all tenants on the current lease and a new lease signed (including an approved application with complete papers from the new tenant).

OBSTRUCTIONS: The sidewalks, entries, halls, and stairways will not be blocked or used for any purposes other than entering or exiting the respective apartments. No recreational equipment or any personal items will be permitted to be placed or kept in the hallways or stairways.

PETS: Tenant(s) is/are not permitted to keep cats or dogs (with the exception of assistance dogs) in the apartment or on the premises. Any animal found on the premises is subject to immediate removal by Management. Animals will not be returned to the tenant or to any neighbor but to the town's animal shelter. In the event that we become aware for any reason of an animal living in an apartment, the tenants shall receive a written notice immediately that they have five (5) days to remove the animal, or eviction proceedings will commence.

PET GUIDELINES: Only one (1) of the following types is permitted per apartment:

- Birds
    - maximum number: two (2)
    - must be maintained **inside** cage at all times
    - no larger than a cockatoo
- Fish and turtles
    - maximum aquarium size: twenty (20) gallons
    - must be maintained properly and on an approved stand

    o    turtles must be inside aquarium

### NO OTHER TYPES OF PETS MAY BE KEPT IN THE APARTMENT.

RECEIVE YOUR FULL DEPOSIT BACK WHEN YOU MOVE: This list is provided as part of your **Lease Agreement** so that you are aware of the costs of property damage and so that you can avoid these expenses and do what is necessary to get your deposit back.

| Cleaning (not done by you) | Bathroom cabinets and floor | $25 |
| | Bathtub/shower and surrounding area | $30 |
| | Carpet cleaning or deodorizing | $150–$250 |
| | Extensive cleaning | $90 |
| | Fireplace | $125 |
| | Kitchen cabinet or countertop | $45 |
| | Kitchen or bathroom floor | $50 |
| | Oven | $30–$100 |
| | Refrigerator | $70–$150 |
| | Stove hood | $30 |
| | Stove top or oven | $30–$100 |
| | Toilet and sink | $20 |
| | Windows (each) | $90 per hour |
| Damages | Remove crayon marks | $75 |
| | Small/large nail hole repair | $55 |
| | Patch sheetrock, compound, and sand | $50–$200 |
| | Replace interior/exterior door | $175–$400 |
| | Replace sliding glass door | $775 |
| | Replace faucets | $195 |
| | Replace bathroom mirror or cabinets | $90–$175 |
| | Replace shower heads | $75 |
| | Replace toilet | $350 |
| | Replace garbage disposal | $275 |
| | Replace countertop | $250–$450 |
| | Repair windowpane | $75–$225 |
| | Replace blinds | $85 |
| | Replace tile/linoleum | $300–$500 |
| Missing items | Replace lightbulb | $3 |
| | Light fixture globe | $20 |
| | Electrical outlet/switch | $15 |
| | Electrical cover plate | $5 |
| | Replace key | $5 |
| | Replace shower curtain | $25 |
| | Replace refrigerator shelf | $35 |
| | Replace oven knob | $16 |

## GENERAL REPAIRS

| | |
|---|---|
| Replace refrigerator shelf | $35 |
| Replace stove/oven knob | $16 |
| Repair ceramic tile | $150 |
| Replace countertop | $275 |
| Replace cutting board | $40 |
| Replace kit/bath cabinet knobs | $10 |
| Replace mirror | $45 |
| Replace medicine cabinet | $100 |
| Replace towel bar | $22 |
| Replace tub/shower enclosure | $195 |
| Regrout bath/shower tiles | $165 |
| Repair porcelain | $135 |
| Replace thermostat | $75 |
| Replace fire extinguisher | $55 |
| Remove junk and debris | $250 |
| Replace doorbell button | $15 |
| Replace doorbell unit | $50 |

## PLUMBING

| | |
|---|---|
| Replace kitchen faucet | $195 |
| Replace bathroom faucet | $195 |
| Replace shower head | $75 |
| Replace toilet tank lid | $45 |
| Replace toilet seat | $35 |
| Replace toilet | $350 |
| Replace garbage disposer | $275 |
| Snake toilet | $45 |
| Clear sewer/cesspool line | $95 |

## ELECTRICAL

| | |
|---|---|
| Replace lightbulb | $3 |
| Replace light fixture globe | $20 |
| Replace light fixture | $55 |
| Replace electrical outlet/switch | $15 |
| Replace electrical cover plate | $5 |

## LOCKS

| | |
|---|---|
| Replace key | $5 |
| Replace door lock | $47 |
| Replace interior doorknob | $28 |
| Replace dead bolt lock | $47 |

## FLOORING

| | |
|---|---|
| Remove carpet stains | $80 |
| Cigarette burn in carpet/floor | $80 |
| Deodorize carpet | $80 |
| Repair carpet | $150 |
| Repair hardwood floor | $95 |
| Refinish hardwood floor | $380 |
| Repair linoleum | $85 |
| Replace bathroom linoleum | $385 |
| Replace kitchen linoleum | $385 |
| Replace floor tile | $75 |
| Replace ceramic tile | $150 |

## WALLS

| | |
|---|---|
| Remove mildew and treat surface | $75 |
| Cover crayon/marker/pen marks | $75 |
| Repair hole in wall | $55 |
| Remove wallpaper | $175 |
| Repaint (per wall/ceiling) | $55 |

## DOORS

| | |
|---|---|
| Repair hole in hollow-core door | $55 |
| Repair forced door damage | $75 |
| Replace door (inside) | $175 |
| Replace door (outside) | $400 |
| Replace sliding glass door | $775 |
| Replace sliding door screen | $65 |

## WINDOWS & TREATMENT

| | |
|---|---|
| Replace window pane | $225 |
| Replace venetian or mini-blind | $85 |
| Replace window shade | $15 |
| Replace window screen | $25 |
| Replace vertical blinds (sliding door) | $175 |

## GROUNDS/EXTERIOR

| | |
|---|---|
| Major yard cleanup | $425 |
| Minor yard cleanup | $225 |
| Mow lawn front and back | $50 |
| Clean gutters | $185 |
| Trim bushes | $35 |

## EXTERMINATING

| | |
|---|---|
| Exterminate for cockroaches | $550 |
| Exterminate for fleas | $375 |

REPAIRS/MAINTENANCE: If you have items in your apartment that need repair, call the office at XXX-XXX-XXXX Monday through Friday between 8:00 a.m. and 4:30 p.m. Please do not wait until a repair becomes an **emergency repair**. **We provide EMERGENCY SERVICE during the hours of 4:30 p.m. and 8:00 a.m., Monday through Friday.** *If on-call staff is called out to your apartment at your request and it is not an emergency, you will be charged for the actual staff time.*

- Tenant agrees to pay for all necessary repairs costing less than $150.
- There is no charge for repair of items in the apartment generated by normal wear and tear or component failure.
- Repair of damages or failures caused by the tenant, family member, or a guest of the tenant will be paid by the tenant.
- No maintenance work, unless of an emergency nature, will be performed on Saturdays, Sundays, or legal holidays. The only requests considered an emergency are those that endanger life, health, or property, not inconvenience.

ROOF ACCESS: Admittance to the roof of the building is restricted to maintenance personnel and antennae licenses and is not otherwise permitted.

SEX OFFENDERS REGISTRY: Management does its best to protect the community against **sex offenders** during the application period. It is the tenant's responsibility to check the Internet and see who may move into the neighborhood.

- Family Watch Dog—http://www.familywatchdog.us/
- NeighborhoodScan.com—https://www.neighborhoodscan.com/
- FBI Sex Offender Registry—http://www.fbi.gov/scams-and-safety/sex-offender-registry
- National Alert Registry—https://orders.nationalalertregistry.com/

SMOKE DETECTOR: Smoke detectors are located in each apartment. Smoke detectors will be checked twice a year during the regular semiannual apartment inspections. It is a violation of state and local laws to disable the smoke detector in any manner or to cover the detector with any material.

SMOKING: Smoking is prohibited in all public areas of the building, including lobbies.

STINK BUGS: Management will contract with a **professional pest exterminator** to determine whether there is a problem and what course of action to take to eliminate the problem. The cost of the extermination contractor and treatment of the apartment will be paid by Management. In addition to the exterminator, the tenant must allow Management to have a contractor caulk all openings to the outside and repair all damaged screens and doors.

TENANT FEEDBACK FORM: The property **Owner** wants to provide you the best level of service possible. In order to achieve that goal, your feedback on what Management does well and areas that can be improved on is most important. Please return the questionnaire as soon as possible after receipt.

TENANT-BILLED SERVICES: Tenant will be billed by Management for additional rent, fees, and charges for all additional services requested that are beyond the scope of the **Lease Agreement**. Payment is expected promptly after receipt.

USE OF PREMISES: Tenant shall occupy and use the premises as a private residence and for no other purpose. Tenant shall not carry on any trade, profession, business, school course of instruction, or entertainment on the premises.

UTILITIES/CABLE: Tenant is responsible for contacting utility/cable companies to transfer services into his or her name.

UTILITY WASTEAGE: Tenant shall not waste electricity, water, heat, air conditioning, or other utilities or services, and agrees to cooperate fully with Management to assure the most effective and energy-efficient operation of the building, and shall not allow the adjustment of any controls. As a condition to claiming any deficiency in the air conditioning or ventilation services provided by Management, tenant shall close any blinds or drapes in the apartment to prevent or minimize direct sunlight.

WATER BEDS: Water beds are not permitted.

WINDOWS: Tenant shall not cover or obstruct any window or door. All window coverings shall have a white or off-white fire-resistant back.

---

If any provision of these **House Rules and Policies** is or should become prohibited under any law, that provision shall be made ineffective without invalidating any remaining provisions.

---

**The undersigned Tenant(s) acknowledge(s) having read and understands the foregoing and receipt of a duplicate original.**

| _____ | _____ | _____ | _____ |
|---|---|---|---|
| Tenant | Date | Tenant | Date |

| _____ | _____ | _____ | _____ |
|---|---|---|---|
| Tenant | Date | Tenant | Date |

Figure OML-9

## Sample: **Tenant Lease – Form**

### Tenant Lease

The Landlord and Tenant agree to lease the Premises at the Rent and for the Term stated on these terms:

| | Lease Term | | Yearly Rent | Security Deposit |
|---|---|---|---|---|
| | **Beginning Date** | **Ending Date** | $ | $ |
| **Date of Lease:** | | | **Rent Per Month** | |
| | | | $ | |
| **Landlord (Lessor)** | | | **Tenant (Lessee)** | |
| | | Name: | | |
| | | Address of Premises: | | |

Section One—Rent

1. The whole amount of rent is due and payable when this Lease is effective. Payment of rent in installments is for Tenant's convenience only. If Tenant defaults, Landlord may give notice to Tenant that Tenant may no longer pay rent in installments and the entire rent for the remaining part of the Term will then be due and payable. Landlord need not give notice to pay rent. Rent must be paid in full and no amount subtracted from it.

2. Tenant will pay Landlord the amount of _____ Dollars ($_____) per month, in advance, as monthly rent for the premises, for the term of this lease. Tenant's first monthly payment is to be paid when Tenant signs this Lease, and each subsequent payment will be due on the first day of each month following for the term of this Lease. Tenant may be required to pay other charges to Landlord under the terms of this Lease. They are to be called "added rent." This added rent is payable as rent, together with the next monthly rent due. Payments will be made at the Landlord's address as stated in this Lease or at any other address Landlord may specify in writing to the Tenant.

3. Installments of rent that are not received by Landlord on the first of the month as required by this Lease are considered late. Late payment of rent constitutes default under the terms of this Lease.
    A. If full payment is not received by the Landlord within ten days of the date of default, Tenant agrees to pay to the Landlord a late fee of Fifty Dollars ($50).
    B. Tenant will pay Landlord an administrative charge of Fifty Dollars ($50) for any check returned to the Landlord for insufficient funds plus, a late fee of Fifty Dollars ($50).
    C. Landlord may require that any future rent payment be in the form of a bank check or money order.

4. Landlord agrees that if Tenant pays the rent and is not in default under this Lease, Tenant may peaceably and quietly have, hold, and enjoy the premises for the term of this lease.

5. Failure by Tenant to make any payment of rent, added rent, or other fee or charge under this Lease constitutes a default.

### Section Two—Security Deposit

1. Tenant has paid Landlord a Security Deposit in the amount stated above, to secure his or her performance of all covenants, agreements, and terms of this Lease. The Security Deposit is subject to the following conditions:

    A. Landlord may use, apply, or retain any or all of the amount of Security Deposit for the payment of any rent due from Tenant; for any administrative, maintenance, or other charges set forth in this Lease; any damages or expenses incurred by Landlord arising from Tenant's failure to comply with any of the terms of this Lease (including but not limited to expenses incurred in re-letting the Premises.)

    B. If, during the Term (or any extension of the term) of this Lease, Landlord is obligated to use all or any part of the Security Deposit in accordance with the terms and conditions of this Lease or any other law or agreement, Landlord shall notify Tenant of the expenditure, in writing, within ten days of its being incurred, and provide along with such notice an itemized list of the charges and expenses, including the reasonable cost of Landlord's own time and labor. Tenant shall have five days in which to deposit with Landlord a sum equal to the amount used, to ensure that the full amount of the Security Deposit is maintained with the Landlord at all times during the term of this Lease.

    C. The use of all or any part of the Security Deposit by Landlord shall not be Landlord's sole remedy in the event of Tenant's default. If the costs of Landlord's expenses and/or damages incurred exceed the total amount of the Security Deposit, Tenant shall pay any excess. **Tenant may not apply the Security Deposit as rent.**

    D. When Tenant has performed all obligations required under this Lease, has paid all rent and any other charges, and has surrendered the Premises, its keys, passes, any other documents or fixtures in the same condition as they were provided at the beginning of the term of this Lease, reasonable wear and tear excepted, Landlord shall return to Tenant any remaining amount of the Security Deposit, together with a fully itemized list of all charges deducted from it, with documentation, within thirty days of the termination of this Lease and the surrender of the Premises.

    E. In the event Landlord's interest in the Premises are sold, transferred, or assigned, Landlord shall notify Tenant of the change in ownership and the name and business address of the new Owner. Landlord shall transfer the Security Deposit to the new Owner and be released from all liability to Tenant. Tenant will look only to the new Owner for return of the Security.

### Section Three—Tenant's Defaults and Landlord's Remedies

1. Landlord may give written notice by certified mail, return receipt requested, to Tenant to correct any of the following defaults:

    A. Failure to pay rent or added rent on time
    B. Failure to pay additional fees or charges as stipulated in this Lease
    C. Improper assignment of Lease, improper subletting all or part of the Premises, or allowing another to use the Premises
    D. Improper conduct by Tenant or other occupant on the Premises
    E. Failure to fully perform any other term in the Lease

2. If Tenant fails to correct the defaults listed above, within five (5) days of receipt of notice, Landlord may cancel the Lease by giving Tenant three (3) days' notice, stating the date the term will end. On that date, the Term and Tenant's rights in this Lease automatically end and Tenant must leave the Premises and give Landlord the keys, and Tenant continues to be responsible for rent, expenses, damages, and losses.

3. If the Lease is canceled, or rent or added rent is not paid on time, or Tenant vacates the Premises, Landlord may in addition to other remedies, take any of the following steps:

    A. Enter the Premises and remove Tenant and any person or property
    B. Use dispossess eviction or other lawsuit method to take back the premises

4. If the Lease is ended or Landlord takes back the Premises, Landlord is entitled to recovery of any damages incurred due to Tenant's default, including but not limited to the cost of relenting the Premises, lost rental under this Lease, and the cost of collections, court cost and reasonable attorney's fees as permitted by law, arising due to Tenant's default, and any other remedy as provided by the laws of the State where this lease is written and signed.

5. Landlord may rerent the Premises and anything in it for any term. Landlord may re-rent for a lower rent and give allowances to the new Tenant. Tenant shall be responsible for Landlord's cost of re-renting.
6. Tenant waives all rights to return to the Premises after possession is given to the Landlord by a Court.

## Section Four—Term Of Lease and Extension

1. Landlord shall not be liable for failure to give Tenant possession of the Premises on the beginning date of the Term. Rent shall be payable as of the beginning of the Term unless Landlord is unable to give possession. In that case, rent shall be payable when possession is available. Landlord will notify Tenant as to the date possession is available. The ending date of the Term will not change.
2. The term of this Lease shall be one year. The Tenant shall have the right to renew this Lease for an additional one (1) year period at a price to be agreed upon by the Landlord and the Tenant.

## Section Five—Condition of Premises

Tenant has examined the condition of the Premises and acknowledges that the Premises are received in good condition and repair and takes the Premises AS IS. Tenant is responsible for all day-to-day maintenance of the Premises as defined in the Rules and Policies for Tenants, including maintaining all devices and appliances in working order. Tenant must keep, and at the end of the term of this Lease, return the Premises and all appliances, system, equipment, furniture, furnishings, and other personal property clean and in good order and repair. Tenant is not responsible for ordinary wear and damage by the elements. If Tenant defaults, Landlord has the right to make repairs and charge the Tenant the cost.

    A. Landlord and Tenant agree that an inventory of furnishings and personal property in the Premises will be taken before occupancy, and each party shall have a signed copy.
    B. Landlord agrees to clean the Premises before Tenant occupies. Tenant agrees to clean the Premises when they are vacated.
    C. Tenant shall not use any nails or adhesives in laying or applying any floor covering. Tenant shall have permission to paint the interior of the premises, with colors approved by the Landlord.
    D. Tenant agrees to make all necessary repairs costing less than $150 at Tenant's own expense. Landlord agrees to make all necessary repairs not caused by Tenant, Tenant's employees, or Tenant's agents costing more than $150 at Landlord's own expense. All structural repairs shall be the responsibility of the Landlord.

## Section Six—Use of Premises

1. The Premises are leased to Lessee exclusively and shall be used as a residence and for no other purpose. The Premises shall be occupied only by the Tenant and any children born to, adopted by, or placed under Tenant's legal care and/or guardianship as listed on the rental application. A violation of any condition of this lease by any guest of Tenant shall be construed as a violation by Tenant.
2. Landlord is not liable for loss, expense, or damage to any person or property unless it is due to Landlord's negligence. Tenant must pay for damages suffered and money spent by Landlord relating to any claim arising from any act or neglect of Tenant. Tenant is responsible for all acts of Tenant's family, employees, guests, and invitees.
3. Tenant agrees that prior to occupancy, Tenant will obtain personal property insurance in a minimal amount of $20,000 and liability insurance in a minimal amount of $100,000 per person per occurrence: $300,000 total. Occupancy by Tenant will be delayed until receipt by Landlord of a satisfactory policy.
    A. Tenant's insurance agent shall furnish Landlord with a Certificate of Insurance, with coverage not less than the amount stated.
    B. Tenant agrees to maintain the policy throughout the duration of tenancy.
    C. Landlord is not liable for Tenant's personal property under any circumstances.
4. Tenant must, at Tenant's cost, promptly comply with all laws, orders, rules, and directions of all Governmental Authorities, Insurance Carriers, or Board of Fire Underwriters or similar group. Tenant may not do anything that may increase Landlord's insurance premiums. If Tenant does, Tenant must pay the increase as added rent.

5. Tenant agrees not to permit the Premises to be used in any manner or for any purpose involving unusual fire or other hazard nor to permit the premises to remain vacant for more than seven (7) days at any one time or for more than twenty-four (24) hours during a time when the outside temperature is below thirty-two degrees, without giving prior notice to the Landlord.

6. Tenant agrees that during periods of vacancy the Tenant will make arrangements to have the Premises checked twice per week in the winter.

7. The premises may not be assigned or sublet by Tenant without written consent of Landlord.

8. Tenant shall not use or allow the Premises to be used for any unlawful or disorderly purpose. The Premises may not be used in any way that represents a material detriment to the health or safety of others. Tenant shall comply with all applicable laws and any Rules and Policies for Tenants established by the Landlord. Tenant shall be provided with a printed copy of the applicable Rules and Regulations at the time this Lease is signed. Landlord has the right to immediately terminate this Lease based on any such violation.

9. If all of the Premises is taken or condemned by a legal authority, the term and tenant's rights shall end as of the date the authority takes title to the Premises. If any part of the Premises is taken, Landlord may cancel this Lease on notice to Tenant setting forth a cancellation date not less than thirty days from the date of the notice. If the Lease is canceled, Tenant must deliver the premises to Landlord on the cancellation date together with all rent due to that date. The entire award for any taking belongs to Landlord. Tenant shall give the Landlord any interest tenant might have to any part of the award and shall make no claims for the value of the remaining part of the term.

## Section Seven—Access, Keys, and Signs

1. Landlord may at reasonable times, with at least forty-eight hours' prior notice, enter the Premises to examine, to make repairs or alterations, and to show it to possible buyers or lenders. Tenant must give to Landlord keys to all locks. Locks may not be changed or additional locks installed without Landlord's consent. Doors must be locked at all times. Windows must be locked when Tenant is out.

2. Sixty (60) days prior to the expiration of this Lease, Landlord shall have the right, upon reasonable notice to Tenant, to show the premises for purchase or lease. Landlord may place the usual "For Rent" or "For Sale" signs upon the Premises.

## Section Eight—Pets

No pets of any kind may be kept in or around the Premises for any purpose. This provision does not apply to companion animals trained and certified to assist a person with a disability.

## Section Nine—Utilities and Maintenance

1. Tenant must pay for the following utilities and services when billed: water, electric, fuel, telephone, gardening, snow removal, exterminating, refuse collection, and any other services contracted by the Tenant. Maintenance service contracts, if any, entered into by the Tenant or listed on the Lease shall be maintained, continued, and paid for by Tenant. These charges will be added rent.

2. Tenant must give Landlord immediate notice in case of fire or other damage to the Premises. Landlord will have the right to repair the damage within a reasonable time or cancel this Lease. If Landlord repairs, Tenant shall pay rent only to the date of the fire or damage and shall start to pay rent again when the Premises become usable. Landlord may cancel the Lease by giving Tenant three days' written notice and provided that said fire renders the premises uninhabitable or unrepairable within a reasonable time. The Term shall be over at the end of the third day, and all rent shall be paid to the date of the damage.

3. Tenant shall keep the grounds neat and clean, the grass cut, leaves raked, ice removed, and snow plowed.

4. Vehicles may be driven or parked only in driveways or in the garage.

5. Tenant agrees to install no major appliances or equipment on the Premises without the written permission of the Landlord.

6. Landlord certifies that the Premises contain all smoke detectors and other devices required by law, and that all such detectors or other devices are in good working order. Tenant is responsible for maintaining such systems.

### Section Ten—Subordination, Severability, and Law

1. This Lease and Tenant's rights are subject and subordinate to all present and future:
   A. Mortgages on the leases or on the premises or on the land.
   B. Agreements securing money paid or to be paid by the lender, under mortgages.
   C. Terms, conditions, renewals, changes of any kind in and extensions of the mortgages or leases or Lender agreements.
   D. Tenant must promptly execute any certificate(s) that Landlord requests to show that this Lease is subject and subordinate.
2. Landlord and Tenant waive trial by a jury in any matter that comes up between the parties under or because of this Lease (except for a personal injury or property damage claim). In a proceeding to get possession of the premises, Tenant shall not have the right to make a counterclaim or setoff.
3. Any dispute arising under this Lease shall be settled by arbitration. Landlord and Tenant shall each choose an arbitrator, and the two arbitrators shall select a third. The findings and award of the three arbitrators thus chosen shall be final and binding on the parties hereto.
4. If any provision of this Lease is or should become prohibited under any law, that provision shall be made ineffective, without invalidating any remaining provisions. The governing law of the jurisdiction in which the Premises are located is incorporated into and supersedes this Lease by reference, and the parties agree to be bound by such law.

### Section Eleven—Miscellaneous

1. The words "Landlord" and "Tenant," as used in this Lease, are construed as including more than one person. All terms and conditions of this Lease are binding on and may be enforced by the parties, their heirs, assigns, executors, administrators, and successors. This Lease represents the entire agreement between Landlord and Tenant. Neither party is bound by any representations made by any party that are not included in this Lease, except that the Rules and Policies for Tenants and Tenant's Application are included by reference.
2. Any bill, statement, or notice must be in writing and delivered or mailed to the tenant at the Premises and to the Landlord at the Address for Notices. It will be considered delivered on the day mailed or if not mailed, when left at the proper address. Any notice must be sent by certified mail. Landlord must send Tenant written notice if Landlord changes the Address for Notices.
3. Whenever Landlord's consent shall be required by the Tenant, Landlord agrees not to unreasonably withhold such consent.
4. Tenant represents that no Broker or Agent brought the property to Tenant's attention and agrees to save the Landlord harmless from the claims of any Broker or Agent.
5. Landlord's failure to enforce any terms of this Lease shall not prevent Landlord from enforcing such terms at a later time.

TENANT IS AWARE THAT HE OR SHE HAS THE RIGHT TO OBTAIN LEGAL COUNSEL PRIOR TO THE EXECUTION OF THIS AGREEMENT. TENANT HAS READ AND UNDERSTANDS THE TENANT RESPONSIBILITIES AND POTENTIAL FINANCIAL LIABILITIES IN THIS **LEASE** AND **RULES AND POLICIES FOR TENANTS** RIDER.

IN WITNESS WHEREOF, the parties hereto have hereunto set their hands and seal this _____ day of _____, 20 _____.

Signed, Sealed, and Delivered in the Presence of:

By: _____          _____
            ([Landlord)                              (Landlord Print Name)

By: _____          _____
         (Tenant Signature)                         (Tenant Print Name)

Figure OMT-1

Sample: **Collection Detail and Checklist – Form CDF**

Property: << *Property* >>                Resident: << *Mr. Tenant* >> and << *Mrs. Tenant* >>

Resident Collection Detail should be prepared for all accounts turned over to collections, in litigation (i.e. small claims or eviction) and for accounts written-off.

| Unit No: | Lease Start Date: | **Amount Due:** | |
|---|---|---|---|
| Monthly Rent: | Move-Out Date: | Rent: | $ |
| Type of Unit: | Lease End Date: | Legal Fees: | |
| Move-in-Date: | Security Deposit: | Other: | |
| | | | |
| | | | |
| | | | |
| | | Subtotal | |
| | | Less Security Deposit | |
| | | Total Due | $ |

**Reason for Action:**
☐ Non-payment
☐ Cause (specify)

☐ Holdover
☐ Skip
☐ Other (explain)

The following items should be included with this file if action is to be taken. (Mark with check when item is complete, "NA" for items not applicable).

☐ Lease or rental agreement.
☐ First notice.          Dated: _____
☐ Second Notice          Dated: _____
☐ Notice to pay or quit. Dated: _____
☐ Documentation of service or delivery
☐ Resident unit ledger.
☐ Move-In/Out inspection.
☐ Documentation regarding personal meetings.
☐ Documentation regarding telephone discussions.
☐ Copies of other related correspondence.
☐ Copies of all legal papers.
☐ Copies of complaints about resident (or memorandum of).

**Recommendation** (note details on separate sheet and attach):

☐ Account to collection agency          Agency:
☐ Eviction *        ☐ Summons served   Dated:
☐ Small Claims *    ☐ Suit filed       Dated:

    * Complete for Eviction or Small Claims Proceedings:

        ☐ Court            _____ , 20
           Date:
        ☐ Judgment:  ☐ Possession   Date:_____ , 20
                ☐ Damages:     Amount: $
                                      _____
                ☐ Dismissed
                ☐ Continuation:  Date:_____ , 20

☐ Accepted Settlement   Amount: $_____
☐ Write-Off Account     Amount: $_____

Notes:

Figure OMT-2

Sample: **Non-Acceptance Letter – Form NAL**

RE:     Reason For Non-Acceptance

Dear << *Applicant's Name* >>:

Your request for tenancy has been denied for the reason(s) indicated below:

| | | | |
|---|---|---|---|
| | Application incomplete. | | Unable to verify employment. |
| | Insufficient credit references. | | Temporary or irregular employment. |
| | Unable to verify credit references. | | Length of employment. |
| | No credit file. | | Insufficient income. |
| | Insufficient credit line. | | Unable to verify income. |
| | Delinquent credit obligations. | | Bankruptcy. |
| | Profit and loss account(s) | | Previous eviction(s). |
| | Excessive obligations. | | Garnishment, foreclosure, or repossession. |
| | We do not offer rentals on the terms you have requested. | | Because of negative information received from a second party. |
| | Charge-offs. | | Too short a period of residence. |
| | Insufficient personal references. | | Other |

☐ Information contained in a consumer credit report obtained from one or more agencies: (See list below.)

☐ A consumer credit report containing insufficient information to meet our requirements was obtained from: (See the list below.)

☐ Information was received from a person or company other than a consumer-reporting agency.  Under Section 615(b) of the Fair Credit Reporting Act you have a right to make a written request to us within 60 days of receiving this letter for a disclosure of the nature of this information.

Because our decision was based on information in your credit history, Section 615(a) of the Fair Credit Reporting Act requires that we provide you with the source of that report. A check mark indicates each agency that provided information about your credit history. The agency took no part in making the decision to reject your application, nor can they explain why the decision was made.

☐          ☐          ☐

| Equifax Credit Information Service | Experian Consumer Assistance | Trans Union Consumer Relations |
|---|---|---|
| PO Box 740241 | PO Box 949 | PO Box 390 |
| Atlanta, GA  30374-2041 | Allen, TX  75002 | Springfield, PA  19064 |
| 800-685-1111 | 800-682-7654 | 800-858-8336 |

You have certain rights under federal law regarding your credit history.  During the sixty-day period that starts _____, you have the right to receive a free copy of your consumer report from any consumer-reporting agency whose name is checked above.

You have a right to dispute the accuracy or completeness of any information contained in your credit report, as furnished by the reporting agency whose name is checked above.  If you believe your file contains errors, is inaccurate or incomplete, call the consumer-reporting agency at their toll-free number listed above, or write to them at the address listed.

You have a right to put into your file a consumer statement up to 100 words in length to explain items in your file.  Trained personnel are available to help you with the consumer statement.

You may have additional rights under the credit reporting or consumer protection laws of your state.  Contact your local consumer protection agency or a state Attorney General's Office.

Sincerely,


_____
*<< Landlord >>, <<Property Owner >>*

Figure OMT-3

Sample: **Notice of Abandonment – Form NLA**

*Note: Must be sent certified mail return receipt.*

To:  << *Mr. Tenant* >> and << *Mrs. Tenant* >>

Re: *(enter state statute)*
    Abandonment of Apartment by Tenant

A recent visit to the premises at which your apartment is located indicated that you apparently have abandoned the apartment.

We will take possession of the apartment if you do not contact us within ten (10) days of receipt of this letter.

Any **items** left in the apartment will be considered abandoned and will be held for thirty (30) days to give you the opportunity to redeem said items. After thirty (30) days, your items will be disposed of. You can contact us by calling << *Office Phone* >> between 9:00 a.m. and 5:00 p.m. or contact us in writing at:

_____

_____

_____

Yours truly,

_____
<< *Landlord* >>, <<*Property Owner* >>

Figure OMT-4

Sample: **Notice of Termination Letter – Form NOT**

### NOTICE OF TERMINATION

To: << *Mr. Tenant* >> and << *Mrs. Tenant* >>,

"Tenant," and to all person(s) occupying the Premises described below:

Premises: << *Rental Address* >> - << *City* >>, << *State* >> << *Zip* >>

(the "Premises").

Re: Lease date _____ between

_____, as Tenant,

and _____, Landlord.

**PLEASE TAKE NOTICE** that pursuant to _____,
the Landlord elects to terminate your tenancy on the grounds that
_____.

**PLEASE TAKE FURTHER NOTICE** that you are hereby required to quit, vacate, and
surrender the **Premises** on/or before _____, that being more than
_____days after the service of this notice upon you, pursuant to the terms of
your lease and applicable law.

**PLEASE TAKE FURTHER NOTICE** that if you fail to vacate or surrender the premises,
the Landlord will commence summary proceeding to evict you.

_____

<< *Landlord* >>, <<*Property Owner* >>  << *Date* >>

Figure OMT-5
_____

Sample:  **Non-Renewal of Lease – Form NRL**


<< *Date* >>


Dear << *Mr. Tenant* >> and << *Mrs. Tenant* >>

According to our records, the lease for your residence will expire on _____, 20__.

Please be advised, this letter serves as our written sixty-day notice, as provided by state law, that we are not going to renew your lease.

I will contact you within ten days so that we can discuss move-out procedures and set up a move-out inspection. In the meantime, if you have any questions, please do not hesitate to call.

Thank you for your cooperation.


Sincerely,


_____
<< *Landlord* >>, <<*Property Owner* >>

Figure TMG-1

Sample: **Master Key Log – Form MKF**

## Master Key Log

| UNIT | | KEY | BOX # | |
|------|------|------|------|------|
| | | | | |
| | | | | |
| | | | | |
| | | | | |
| | | | | |
| | | | | |
| | | | | |
| | | | | |
| | | | | |
| | | | | |
| | | | | |
| | | | | |
| | | | | |
| | | | | |
| | | | | |
| | | | | |
| | | | | |
| | | | | |
| | | | | |
| | | | | |
| | | | | |
| | | | | |
| | | | | |
| | | | | |
| | | | | |
| | | | | |
| | | | | |
| | | | | |

Figure TMG-2

Sample: **Notice of Intent to Enter Dwelling Unit – Form NIE**

# NOTICE OF INTENT TO ENTER DWELLING UNIT

<< *Mr. Tenant* >> and << *Mrs. Tenant* >>

<< *Rental Address* >>
<< *City* >>, << *State* >> << *Zip* >>

THIS NOTICE is to inform you that on _____, at approximately _____a.m./p.m., the landlord or the landlord's agent will enter the premises for the following reason:

[___] To make or arrange for the following repairs or improvements:

_____

_____

☐ To show the premises to
    ☐ a prospective tenant or purchaser;
    ☐ workers or contractors regarding the above repair or improvement; or
    ☐ other. _____

You are, of course, welcome to be present. If you have any questions or if the date or time is inconvenient, please notify me promptly at the following number << *Office Phone* >>

<< *Landlord* >>, <<*Property Owner* >>   << *Date* >>

Figure TMG-3

Sample: **Request for Service – Form RSF**

| | **Maintenance Request & Work Order** |
|---|---|
| | **REQEST FOR SERVICE** |
| Building:<br>Unit:<br>Resident: | Start Time: |
| Address: | Finish Time: |
| Phone: | |
| Date: | Total Hours: |

**Work Requested** (Job Description)

| |
|---|
| |
| |
| |
| |

**Charge To:** (circle one)    **TENANT    OWNER    MANAGEMENT**

**Assigned To:**

| **Work Completed:** | | | | |
|---|---|---|---|---|
| | | | | |
| | | | | |
| | | | | |
| | | | | |
| | | | | |
| **Tenant authorization** | | | | |
| | | | | |
| | | | | |

Figure TMG-4

## Sample:  **Tenant Exit Letter – Form TEL**

*<< Date >>*

*<< Mr. Tenant >>* and *<< Mrs. Tenant >>*

We hope you have enjoyed living here. In order that we may mutually end our relationship on a positive note, this move-out letter describes how we expect your apartment to be left and what our procedures are for returning your security deposit.

Basically, we expect you to leave your rental unit in the same condition it was in when you moved in, except for normal wear and tear. To refresh your memory on the conditions of the unit when you moved in, I have attached a copy of the **Landlord/Tenant Checklist** you signed at the beginning of your tenancy. We will be using the same form to inspect your unit when you leave.

Specifically, here is a list of items you should thoroughly clean before vacating:

- ☐ Floors
- ☐       Sweep and dry mop wood floors
- ☐       Vacuum carpets and rugs (shampoo if necessary)
- ☐       Mop kitchen and bathroom floors
- ☐ Walls, baseboards, ceilings, and built-in shelves
- ☐ Kitchen cabinets, countertops and sink, stove and oven (inside and out)
- ☐ Refrigerator: empty of food, clean inside and out, and turn it off with the door left open
- ☐ Bathtubs, showers, toilets, and plumbing fixtures
- ☐ Doors, windows, and window coverings
- ☐ Other:

_____

If you have any questions as to the type of cleaning we expect, please let me know. Please do not leave ***anything*** behind—that includes bags of garbage, clothes, food, newspapers, furniture, your personal appliances, dishes, plants, cleaning supplies, or other items. Please be sure you have disconnected phone and utility services, canceled all newspaper subscriptions, and sent the Post Office a change-of-address form.

Once you have cleaned your unit and removed all your belongings, please call me at (XXX) XXX-XXXX to arrange for a walk-through inspection and to return all keys. Please be prepared to give me your forwarding address where we may mail your security deposit.

It is our policy to return all deposits to an address you provide within one month after you move out. If any deductions are made for past-due rent or because the unit is damaged or not sufficiently clean, they will be explained in writing. If you have any questions, please contact me at (XXX) XXX-XXXX.

Sincerely,


_____
*<< Landlord >>, <<Property Owner >>*

P.S.   We are enclosing "**Resident Exit Interview**" for you to complete at your convenience and mail back to us in the enclosed stamped envelope.

Sample: **Guide-lines for Return of Security – Form GLF**

## Guidelines for Return of Security Deposit

| Property: | Unit: |
|---|---|

| Resident: | Lease End Date: | Move-Out Date: |
|---|---|---|

Security deposit(s) will be refunded provided the resident has complied with all provisions of the lease, including length of lease, proper notice to vacate (sixty days), rent and other monies due paid through date of move out, keys returned, and charges paid for any damage (other than normal wear) to the unit or property.

The following guidelines will be used to determine the return of the security deposit:

**CARPETS**

☐ Vacuumed and cleaned*

☐ Stains and odors removed

☐ Rips and holes repaired

**WALLS AND CEILINGS**

☐ Holes repaired

☐ Torn surfaces repaired

☐ Stains removed

☐ Original color restored
(unless change authorized)

**KITCHEN**

☐ Refrigerator defrosted
and cleaned

☐ Dishwasher cleaned

☐ Oven cleaned

☐ Cabinets cleaned

☐ Sink scoured

☐ All foodstuffs and paper
removed

☐ Countertops cleaned

☐ Floor swept and mopped

**BATHROOM(S)**

☐ Sink cleaned

☐ Shower and tub cleaned

☐ Toilet cleaned

☐ Medicine cabinet cleaned

**WINDOWS**

☐ Panes and sashes cleaned

☐ Sills and framework cleaned

☐ Ledges cleaned

**ACCESSORIES**

☐ Ice trays present

☐ Traverse rods present

☐ Window screens present

☐ Light fixtures cleaned

**OTHER**

☐ Closets cleaned

☐ All trash removed

☐ Keys returned

☐ Mirror cleaned

☐ Floor swept and mopped

☐ Trash and personal effects
removed

*Receipt to be given to landlord.

Notes:

_____

_____

_____

_____

Figure TMG-6

## Sample: **Tenant Exit Letter – Form TEL**

*<< Date >>*

Dear *<< Mr. Tenant >>* and *<< Mrs. Tenant >>*

We hope you have enjoyed living here. In order that we may mutually end our relationship on a positive note, this move-out letter describes how we expect your unit to be left, and what our procedures are for returning your security deposit.

We expect you to leave your rental unit in the same condition it was in when you moved in, except for normal wear and tear. To refresh your memory on the conditions of the unit when you moved in, I have attached a copy of the Landlord/Tenant Checklist you signed at the beginning of your tenancy. We will be using the same form to inspect your unit when you leave.

Specifically, here is a list of items you should thoroughly clean before vacating:

- ☐ Floors
    - ☐ Sweep wood floors and dry mop.
    - ☐ Vacuum carpets and rugs (shampoo if necessary).
    - ☐ Mop kitchen and bathroom floors.
- ☐ Walls, baseboards, ceilings and built-in shelves.
- ☐ Kitchen cabinets, countertops and sink, stove and oven - inside and out.
- ☐ Refrigerator - empty it of food, clean inside and out, and turn it off with the door left open.
- ☐ Bathtubs, showers, toilets and plumbing fixtures.
- ☐ Doors, windows and window coverings.
- ☐ Other:

If you have any questions as to the type of cleaning we expect, please let me know. Please do not leave *anything* behind, that includes bags of garbage, clothes, food, newspapers, furniture, appliances, dishes, plants, cleaning supplies or other items. Please be sure you have disconnected phone and utility services, canceled all newspaper subscriptions, and sent the Post Office a change-of-address form.

Once you have cleaned your unit and removed all your belongings, please call me at (XXX) XXX-XXXX to arrange for a walk-through inspection and to return all keys. Please be prepared to give me your forwarding address where we may mail your security deposit.

It is our policy to return all deposits either in person or at an address you provide within one month after you move-out. If any deductions are made for past due rent, or because the unit is damaged or not sufficiently clean, they will be explained in writing. If you have any questions, please contact me at (XXX) XXX-XXXX.

Sincerely,

_____
*<< Landlord >>*, *<<Property Owner >>*

P.S.     We are enclosing "**Resident Exit Interview**" for you to complete at your convenience and mail back to us in the enclosed stamped envelope.

Figure TMG-7

Sample: **Resident Exit Interview – Form EIF**

### RESIDENT EXIT INTERVIEW (CONFIDENTIAL)

| Property: | Resident: |
|---|---|
| | |

| Number Living in Unit: | Length of Occupancy: | Unit No.: |
|---|---|---|
| | | |

We are sorry you are leaving. Whenever residents move, we welcome comments, criticisms, and suggestions to help us offer the best possible apartment rental. Please indicate your opinion by checking the appropriate columns—rate items from 1 (poor) to 5 (excellent), with 3 being average. Check N if you have no basis for judgment or an item is not applicable. We would appreciate you answering the survey below and returning it in the envelope provided. Space has been provided for additional comments.

| Item | 1 | 2 | 3 | 4 | 5 | N | Comments |
|---|---|---|---|---|---|---|---|
| **GENERAL APPEARANCE** | | | | | | | |
| Building | | | | | | | |
| Property entrance | | | | | | | |
| Landscaping | | | | | | | |
| Driveways | | | | | | | |
| Parking | | | | | | | |
| Building exterior | | | | | | | |
| Walks | | | | | | | |
| Recreational facilities | | | | | | | |
| **Apartment** | | | | | | | |
| Entrance | | | | | | | |
| Halls/Stairs | | | | | | | |

| | | | | | | | |
|---|---|---|---|---|---|---|---|
| Floor plan | | | | | | | |
| Living room | | | | | | | |
| Dining room | | | | | | | |
| Kitchen | | | | | | | |
| Appliances | | | | | | | |
| Cabinets | | | | | | | |
| Bedroom(s) | | | | | | | |
| Bathroom(s) | | | | | | | |
| Doors | | | | | | | |
| Floors | | | | | | | |
| Walls | | | | | | | |
| Windows | | | | | | | |
| Closets | | | | | | | |
| Ceilings | | | | | | | |
| Light fixtures | | | | | | | |
| Electrical outlets | | | | | | | |
| Heating | | | | | | | |
| Air conditioning | | | | | | | |
| Hot water | | | | | | | |

Have you found our staff to be knowledgeable, courteous, and cooperative?

Please explain: _____

_____

_____

Have you been satisfied with the handling of your requests for service? ☐ Yes ☐ No

Was the quality of the work, response time, and staff courtesy satisfactory? ☐ Yes ☐ No

Please explain: _____

_____

_____

What are your principal reasons for moving?

☐ Purchasing a house                        ☐ Rent increase

☐ Renting a house                           ☐ Moving out of area

☐ Moving to a larger apartment              ☐ Moving to property with better facilities/amenities,
                                              please specify:

☐ Moving to smaller apartment               _____

☐ Dissatisfied with Owner                   _____

☐ Other, please specify:

                                            _____

Is there anything that we could have done that would have increased the likelihood that you would have
continued your residency here? _____

_____

Would you recommend this apartment to others? ☐ Yes ☐ No

Please explain: _____

_____

---

Other comments or suggestions:

_____

_____

Thank you for your cooperation in completing this survey.

We value your opinions as we continually explore

ways to improve our service.

Figure TMP-1

## Sample: **Bad Check Letter – Form BCL**

<< *Date* >>

Re: Bad Check

Dear << *Mr. Tenant* >> and << *Mrs. Tenant* >>

Please be advised that your check, number ____, dated the __ of ____, 20 __, and payable to
_____ drawn upon your account at _____, has not been honored by the bank.

In accordance with _____ state law, you have **eight days** from receipt of this notice to tender payment for the full amount of the above-described check, plus a service charge of fifty dollars ($50). According to state statutes, the issuance of a check with insufficient funds is a

Class D felony if the issued check is over $1,000;

Class A misdemeanor if more than $500 but less than $1,000;

Class B misdemeanor if more than $250 but less than $500; or

Class C misdemeanor if less than $250.

A felony is punishable by more than one year of imprisonment plus financial restitution, and a misdemeanor is punishable by less than a year of imprisonment with financial restitution. All offenses provide for a permanent criminal record and public disclosure.

It is not our objective to prosecute you for the dishonored check; however, we are looking for immediate and complete restitution. Your payment must be made by **money order** to _____ at _____ within the time stated above. Personal or certified checks will not be accepted.

Additionally, until we receive the money order covering your bad check and bad check processing cost, you must pay a late fee of $_____ (10 percent of monthly rent), plus a daily late charge $_____ (1 percent of monthly rent). These additional fees will be billed to you before your next monthly rent payment is due.

If you have any question about this letter, please call **today**. Thank you for your prompt attention to this matter.

Sincerely,

_____
<< *Landlord* >>, <<*Property Owner* >>

Figure TMP-2

Sample: **Rent Late Warning and Excuses – Form TWE**

Dear Resident:

Your rent is due on the first day of the month. I am sure you fully understand that we must start eviction proceeding instantly once a payment is late (no matter the reason) and report your late payment to both local and national tenant/credit reporting agencies. We still request, however, that you submit your reason for late payment for our records. For your convenience and to avoid lengthy explanation, you may simply check the appropriate reason below and submit this form with your late payment. We hope this form and your payment will be received before you are evicted. Even better, your payment will always arrive on time, and you will not need this form.

***I'm sorry my rent is late, but...***

|  | | |
|---|---|---|
|  | A. | The check that I have been waiting for did not come in the mail or was late. |
|  | B. | I was in the hospital/jail, and I could not get to you. |
|  | C. | I missed a week's work because I had to take care of my sick mother/son/daughter. |
|  | D. | I had to have some teeth pulled, and the dentist would not start work until I gave some money. |
|  | E. | I was in an automobile accident, and I won't have any money until my attorney works things out with the other guy's insurance. |
|  | F. | I had my wallet stolen when this guy jumped me on my way to the bank/post office/my office. |
|  | G. | Someone broke into my apartment and took my money. No, I didn't file a police report. Should I? |
|  | H. | I had to have my car fixed so I could get to work so I could pay you. |
|  | I | My mother/sister/uncle hasn't mailed me my money yet. |
|  | J. | I couldn't find your address. I put the wrong address on the envelope. |
|  | K. | I got laid off from my job, and I won't get unemployment for a couple of weeks. |
|  | L. | I was unable to get a money order, and I know you didn't want me to send cash. |
|  | M. | You didn't come by when I had the money. |
|  | N. | My husband/wife/boyfriend/girlfriend/roommate left, and I didn't have all the money. |
|  | O. | I told my friend to bring it or send it to you while I was out of town. |
|  | P. | I haven't received my tax refund yet. |
|  | Q. | I got a new job, and I had to work three weeks before I got my first check. |
|  | R. | My car is broken, and I didn't have a ride to your office/the post office. |
|  | S. | I had to help my brother/sister/friend who had a serious problem. |
|  | T. | My grandmother died, and I had to go to the funeral. |
|  | U. | I didn't have a stamp/I forgot to put a stamp on the envelope. |
|  | V. | The check's in the mail. Didn't you get it? |
|  | W. | I ran out of checks. |
|  | X. | I'm dead! |
|  | Y. | Please briefly if your excuse is not listed above: |

Sincerely,

_____

*<< Landlord >>, <<Property Owner >>*

Figure TMP-3

Sample: **Payment Applies to Arrears – Form PAR**

*<< Date >>*

RE: Arrear Balance

Dear *<< Mr. Tenant >>* and *<< Mrs. Tenant >>*

We have received your payment of $_____ by (check #) (money order #) _____
on _____ 20    .
Please be advised that:

- This payment and all future payments will be applied on arrears balances and/or for use and occupancy. This payment and all future payments are not accepted as rent.
- The Landlord is not relinquishing or waiving his rights under the notice of termination served upon you or under the lease. Rather, all of the Landlords' rights in connection with said notice and said lease are hereby reserved.
- Your landlord does not intend to create a new tenancy by acceptance of this payment, or by the acceptance of this amount, or by the acceptance of all future payments, since they are not accepted as rent but on the account of arrearage and/or for us of occupancy only.
- This may be the last notice that you will receive concerning future payments. All future payments will be accepted as stated above regardless of any notation on your check or money order, and regardless of any further delivery of letters similar to this one.

_____
*<< Landlord >>, <<Property Owner >>*

cc:  Resident File
     Legal

**169**

Figure TMP-4

Sample: **Non-Performance Letter – Form NPL**

# Non-Performance Letter to Bureau

## Alert! Your Immediate Action Is Required.
## Poor Performance to Be Reported.

<< *Date* >>

Dear << *Mr. Tenant* >> and << *Mrs. Tenant* >>

The poor performance of items marked below are about to be reported to a nationwide tenant reporting agency. The function of the agency receiving this information is to track and maintain records on tenants, including information on your credit history and your performance as a tenant. This information is available to future landlords, lenders, and creditors who request it. This notification is sent to you to avoid this action from being necessary, if you respond immediately!

**The following POOR PERFORMANCE is to be reported unless you take responsive action**

| | | | | |
|---|---|---|---|---|
| 1. | ___ | Unpaid rent | 9. ___ | Excessive junk outside |
| 2. | ___ | Late rent payment | 10. ___ | Rental upkeep violation |
| 3. | ___ | Return check | 11. ___ | Damaged property |
| 4. | ___ | Unpaid repair bill | 12. ___ | Health or safety hazard/violation |
| 5. | ___ | Excessive noise | 13. ___ | Threats to Landlord/Others |
| 6. | ___ | Unauthorized occupant(s) | 14. ___ | |
| 7. | ___ | Unauthorized pet(s) | 15. ___ | |
| 8. | ___ | Unauthorized vehicle | 16. ___ | |

If you satisfactorily resolve the situation(s) described above with the landlord within seventy-two hours from the date indicated at the top of this page, this information will not be reported to the national tenant-reporting agency at this time. To satisfactorily resolve this matter, _____

The reputation you establish here will be with you for many years to come.

Sincerely,

_____
<< *Landlord* >>, <<*Property Owner* >>

NOTE TO TENANT(S): To respond to or dispute this report, please call << *Office Phone* >>

Figure TMP-5

## Sample: **Resident Damage Letter – Form RDA**

*<< Date >>*

RE:  Resident Damage

Dear *<< Mr. Tenant >>* and *<< Mrs. Tenant >>*

This is a bill for work and/or repairs dated _____, 20___ for:

| | | |
|---|---|---|
| $ | | Lost apartment keys/lockout during work hours<br>Labor/materials |
| | | Lost apartment keys/lockout after work hours<br>Labor/materials |
| | | Changed apartment lock(s) at request of the resident<br>Labor/materials |
| | | Broken, torn, or missing screen<br>Labor/materials |
| | | Found and removed an object from the toilet and/or sink<br>Cost:  $ _____ |
| | | Replaced shade (s) /blinds<br>Cost:  $ _____ |
| | | Broken hollow-core door in unit(labor and materials)<br>Cost:  $ _____ |
| | | Cost:  $ _____ |
| | | Other damage:<br>Cost:  $ _____ |

We are billing you because the repairs ___needed/made___ are considered more than what we consider as normal wear and tear work.

You owe $ _____ for materials and $ _____ for labor, totaling $ _____

Please make your payment by money order only to:

If the amount is not paid by _____, 20___, we have the right to pursue the amount trough legal means.  This date may provide you with a maximum of 30 days to pay, depending upon the amount owed.  If you have any questions concerning this bill, feel free to contact the Landlord at *<< Office Phone >>* or by email _____

_____
*<< Landlord >>, <<Property Owner >>*

cc:  Resident File

Figure TMP-6

Sample: **Incident Report– Form IRF**

| Date of the incident: | Time of the incident: |
|---|---|
| Incident location: | Apartment: |
| Who was involved? | |
| What happened? | |
| Any witnesses? If yes, who? | |
| Where do they live? | |
| Insurance adjuster contacted? | |
| Fire department contacted? | |
| Police department contacted? | |
| Action or follow up? | |
| Who prepared this report? | |

Figure TMP-7

Sample:  **Use and Occupancy – Form UOL**

*<< Date >>*

RE:  Use and Occupancy

Dear *<< Mr. Tenant >>* and *<< Mrs. Tenant >>*

It has been brought to my attention that on __day_____, ___date_____ you had a party in your apartment that lasted until 3 A.M.  Your visitors were very loud as they left the building, shouting and arguing in the vestibule and front doorway.

This is the second time you have had a party in the past two months that has lasted until the early morning hours and that your visitors were excessively loud while leaving the building.  I thought we agreed the last time we spoke that you would cooperate with the other tenants in the building by ending your parties by midnight.

Section   Article of your lease states that "excessive noise that disturbs the quiet enjoyment of other tenants is not allowed".  Please review your lease and consider your neighbors in the future by asking your visitors to keep their voices low when the leave your apartment and the building.  Please respect our agreement to end any party in your apartment by midnight.

I hope that this letter will not be necessary to write again.  If you wish to discuss this with me, I can be reached at *<< Office Phone >>*

Sincerely,

_____
*<< Landlord >>*

cc:  Resident File
     Legal

Figure TMP-8

## Sample: **Notice— Form LRN**

To: << *Mr. Tenant* >> and << *Mrs. Tenant* >>
    Tenant(s) in possession

Address: << *Rental Address* >>
         << *City* >>, << *State* >> << *Zip* >>

You are hereby notified that you have violated or failed to perform the following terms in your rental agreement, which states that resident(s) agree to

     a.   pay rent on the first of the month;
     b.   not play loud music; or
     c.   _____

2.   You are in violation of that provision for the following reason(s):
     a.   Section _____
     b.   Section _____
     c.   Section _____

3.   You must perform or correct this violation within _____ days after service of this notice. The violation can be corrected by immediately doing the following:

     _____

     If you fail to perform or correct the terms of the rental agreement within the specified time, you must vacate and deliver possession of the premises to the landlord.

4.   If you fail to correct or vacate within _____ days, legal proceeding will be initiated against you to recover possession, rent owed, damages, court costs, and attorney fees.

5.   It is not our intention to terminate the rental agreement. However, all tenants must follow guidelines stated in the agreement. If you are unable to comply, the landlord elects to declare a forfeiture of your rental agreement. You will also be subject to forfeit any security deposit given by you to cover any costs you are still liable for, and the landlord reserves the right to pursue collection of any future rental losses. We may be contacted at _____.

Thank you for your prompt cooperation in correcting this matter.


_____

<< *Landlord* >>, <<*Property Owner* >>  << *Date* >>

Figure TMR-1

## Sample:  **Pay Rent in Arrears – Form AML**

*<< Date >>*

RE:  Agreement to Pay Rent Arrears:

I (We) << *Mr. Tenant* >> and << *Mrs. Tenant* >>, living at the above referenced address, acknowledge that my (our) rent is in arrears this date in a total amount of $_____

I agree to pay $ _____ (per month) or $ _____ per (per week) on my arrears until my rent arrears is paid in full.

I also agree to continue to pay my regular monthly rent of $_____ by the 1st business day of each month.

I understand that the landlord still reserves the legal right to continue the eviction action at his discretion.  ***All monies received will be for use and occupancy only as long as I have a rent balance.***  The Landlord reserves his legal right throughout this agreement, if not broken by the resident.

_____          _____
(Resident name)                              (date)     (Co-Resident name)          (date)

_____
*<< Landlord >>, <<Property Owner >> << Date >>*

cc:  Resident File
     Legal

Figure TMR-2

Sample: **Rent Increase Letter – Form RIL**

*<< Date >>*

To:     *<< Mr. Tenant >>* and *<< Mrs. Tenant >>*
        *<< Rental Address >>*
        *<< City >>*, *<< State >> << Zip >>*

Re:  Rent

**Current Rent**          **Market Value**          **New Rent**

$ _____          $ _____          $ _____

Dear Resident:

This letter is to notify you that there will be a change to the terms of tenancy under which you occupy the property at the above address. As of the following date _____, your rent will be adjusted by $ ____ per month. The new rent amount will be $____ per month, payable in advance. The rent increase is due in part to the following reasons:

_____

*<< Landlord >>, <<Property Owner >>*

P.S. To help keep future rental increases to a minimum, your cooperation continues to be appreciated with on-time payments.

Figure TMR-3

Sample: **Security Deposit Accounting – Form SDA**

| SECURITY DEPOSIT ACCOUNTING | | | | | |
|---|---|---|---|---|---|
| Property: | | | | Unit: | |
| Resident: | | | New Mailing Address: | | |
| Lease Start Date: | | | | | |
| **ACCOUNTING** | | | | | |
| **DEPOSITS** | | | | | |
| | Security Deposit: | | $00,000.00 | | |
| | Pet Deposit: | | $0,000.00 | | |
| | Other: | | $0,000.00 | | |
| | | | $0,000.00 | | |
| | | Key: | $0,000.00 | | |
| | | | $0,000.00 | | |
| | | Sub-Total: | **$0,000.00** | | |
| | | Interest: | $0,000.00 | | |
| | | | **$00,000.00** | **Total Credit** | |
| **DEDUCTIONS** | | | | | |
| | Current Amount Due: | | | | |
| | Rent: | $000.00 | day @ | days | $0,000.00 |
| | Other: | | | | $0,000.00 |
| | | | Sub-Total: | **$0,000.00** | |
| **Termination Fees** | | | | | |
| | | Inadequate Notice: | $0,000.00 | | |
| | | Termination Fee: | $0,000.00 | | |
| | | Sub-Total: | **$0,000.00** | | |
| **Other Charges** | | | | | |
| | | Damages (from move-in/move-out inspection): | $0,000.00 | | |
| | | Sub-Total: | **$0,000.00** | | |
| | | | **$00,000.00** | **Total Deductions** | |
| | **TOTAL DUE RESIDENT (LANDLORD)** | | | **$00,000.00** | |

If Total Due is to Resident, check is enclosed. If Total due is to Owner, this amount is due upon receipt of this notice. To avoid further notices, collection, and adverse credit reports, tis amount should be paid immediately.
Make check payable to:
Mail to:
If you have any questions or need additional information regarding this accounting, please contact the Property Manager.
Sincerely,

_____, Asset Manager

*<< Company >>*

DATE:

Figure TMR-4

Sample: **Residential Rent Roll – Form RRR**

| RESIDENTIAL RENT ROLL | | | | | | | | |
|---|---|---|---|---|---|---|---|---|
| Property Name: | | | | | | | | |
| Property Address: | | | | | | | | |
| City: | | | | State: | | | Zip: | |
| | | | | | | | | |
| APT. | TENANT | Sq. Ft. | BR | BA | CURRENT RENT | ORIGINAL OCCUPANCY | LEASE EXPIRATION | |
| | | | | | | | | |
| | | | | | | | | |
| | | | | | | | | |
| | | | | | | | | |
| | | | | | | | | |
| | | | | | | | | |
| | | | | | | | | |
| | | | | | | | | |
| | | | | | | | | |
| | | | | | | | | |
| | | | | | | | | |
| | | | | | | | | |
| | | | | | | | | |
| | | | | | | | | |
| | | | | | | | | |
| | | | | | | | | |
| | | | | | | | | |
| | | | | | | | | |
| | | | | | | | | |
| | | | | | | | | |
| | | | | | | | | |
| | | | | | | | | |
| | | | | | | | | |
| | | | | | | | | |
| | | | | | | | | |
| | | | | | | | | |
| | | | | | | | | |
| | | | | | | | | |

# APPENDIX B

## CONSERVATION

# CONSERVATION

Conservation should be an important factor in all the decisions that we make on investment property. That is, during its acquisition we should take note of all available opportunities to implement conservation methods, so that we can implement them upon ownership.

Additionally, conservation means using energy efficient equipment and appliances which saves money on utility bills and protects our climate by helping prevent harmful carbon pollution, and reducing other greenhouse gases.

## Conservation Upgrades

Solar-powered, roof-mounted exhaust fan: The unit is completely powered by the sun and will help remove excess heat and moisture from your attic to protect your roofing system from premature deterioration. The solar-powered unit requires no wiring, uses no electricity, and works well with existing intake vents to help lower the temperature in the attic. Each fan comes with a built-in humidistat and thermostat.

Solar-powered daylighting systems: These are an energy-efficient way to provide natural light during the daytime to common-use areas. Systems are engineered to work with all roof types and to go around rafters and joists so they require no structural changes. The circular design allows rain and debris to bypass the rooftop dome, making them virtually maintenance-free.

Retrofit existing lighting fixtures with energy-efficient LED fixtures. (Outdoor: standard floods, area floods, wall packs, and canopy fixtures. Indoor: flat panel, troffer, motion-sensor, and LED bulbs) LED lights are extremely energy efficient and consume up to 90 percent less power than incandescent bulbs. Also, due to the long life of the LEDs (ten times longer than fluorescent and 133 times longer than incandescent bulbs), there is a substantial saving in maintenance and replacement costs.

The installation of timers on common-area lighting and motion detectors in laundry room and storage areas.

The installation of water-saving device on the kitchen faucets, water closets, lavatories, and shower heads.

The conversion of domestic hot waters to an on-demand (tankless) hot water system.

## Energy Performance

Heat gain and loss: Windows, doors, and skylights can gain and lose heat through direct conduction through the glass, frame, and/or door and air leakage through and around them. These properties can be measured and rated according to the following energy performance values:

- U-factor: This is the rate at which a window, door, or skylight conducts non-solar heat flow. The lower the U-factor, the more energy efficient the product.

- Solar heat gain coefficient (SHGC): This is the fraction of solar radiation admitted through a window, door, or skylight either transmitted directly and/or absorbed and subsequently released as heat inside the home. The lower the SHGC, the less solar heat it transmits and the greater its shading ability.

- Air leakage: This is the rate of movement around a window, door, or skylight in the presence of a specific pressure difference against it. A product with a low air leakage rating is tighter than one with a high air leakage rating.

Energy Star distinguishes energy-efficient products that may cost more to purchase than standard models but will pay you back in lower energy bills within a reasonable time. Caution: not all Energy Star products qualify for a tax credit.

## Tax Credits

Existing residential buildings can qualify for federal tax credits. The tax credit is 30 percent of the product or fixtures cost, with no upper limit. Verify eligibility and expiration on the federal website.

- Geothermal heat pumps: These are similar to ordinary heat pumps but use ground water instead of outside air to provide heating, air conditioning, and, in most cases, hot water. These pumps use the earth's natural heat and are the most efficient technology available. Tax credits include installation costs.

- Solar energy systems (photovoltaic systems): The tax credit is only available for the residence (no swimming pools or hot tubs). The system must meet applicable fire and electrical code requirements. The tax credit includes installation costs.

- Solar panels (photovoltaic systems): This is a system that uses solar cells that capture light energy from the sun and convert it directly into electricity. The basic system's components consist of solar panels, inverter charger, charge controller solar batteries, and other miscellaneous pieces to complete the photovoltaic system, including junction boxes, cabling, and couplers.

| | Tax incentive criteria | Federal tax credit | Details |
|---|---|---|---|
| **Solar photovoltaics (solar panels)** | Photovoltaic systems must provide power to residence claiming the credit | Thirty percent of total system cost. No cap | Placed into service before 12/31/2019 |
| | | Twenty-six percent of total system cost. No cap | Placed into service after 12/31/2019 and before 1/1/2020 |
| | | Twenty-two percent of total system cost. No cap | Placed into service after 1/1/2021 and before 1/1/2022 |
| | | | IRS Tax Form 5695 |
| **Insulation** | Meets 2009 IECC and Amendments | Thirty percent, up to $1,500 maximum | Primary function is insulation. For example, vapor retarders are covered; siding does not qualify. Must have at least a two-year warranty |
| | | | IRS Tax Form 5695 |
| **Windows and doors** | Visit Energy Star Federal Incentives for complete details | Thirty percent up to $1,500 maximum. $200 cap removed | Not all ENERGY STAR labeled windows, doors, and skylights qualify for tax credit |
| | | | IRS Tax Form 5695 |
| **Conventional HVAC** | Central AC, air source heat pumps, natural gas or propane furnace, gas, propane, or oil hot water boiler, advanced main air circulating fan | Thirty percent up to $1,500 maximum | Visit Energy Star Federal Incentives for complete details |
| | | | IRS Tax Form 5695 |
| **Roofing** | Energy Star Qualified Metal and Asphalt Roofs | Thirty percent up to $1,500 maximum | Visit Energy Star Federal Incentives for complete details |
| | | | IRS Tax Form 5695 |

# APPENDIX C

## ABBREVIATIONS AND FORMULAS
## COMMONLY USED WORDS AND PHRASES

## ABBREVIATIONS and FORMULAS

| | DESCRIPTION |
|---|---|
| ACF | Annual Cash Flow |
| ADS | Annual Debt Service. All bank loan payments made in one year. |
| ARR | Annual Debt Service. All bank loan payments made in one year. |
| Basis Point | A basis point is equal to $1/100^{th}$ of 1%, 1 percent equal's 100 basis points, and 0.01 percent equals 1 basis point. |
| CAP | Capitalization Rate - Rate of return on purchase price. Buyers look for high CAP rates. |
| CCR-B | Shows remaining cash after all operating expenses and mortgages are paid compared to the initial amount of capital invested to acquire the property. CCR-B = ACF/Initial Cash Investment |
| CF | Cash Flow (CF=PGI-Vacancy-Expenses-Debt Service) |
| CFBT | Cash Flow Before Taxes CFBT=NOI-DS |
| DCR | Debt Service Ratio |
| DS | Debt Service (PI times 12) |
| DSCR | Debt Service Coverage Ratio or Debt Coverage Ratio is the ability to cover the monthly mortgage payment from cash generated by the rental property. (DSCR=NOI/ADS) |
| GIM | Gross Income Multiplier (GIM=MP/PGI) |
| GRM | Gross Rent Multiplier is another way to value and compare apartment properties |
| IRR | The discount rate at which the net present value of all future cash flow is zero. |
| LTV | Loan-to-Value - The maximum loan amount of any acquisition. |
| MAD | Maximum Annual Debt: (MAD=NOI/DSCR |
| MP | Market Price |
| NOI | Net Operating Income is the net cash generated before mortgage payments and taxes. When the NOI is expected to grow, the CAP Rate is Low. |
| PGI | Potential Gross Income - The maximum yearly income you would receive if the property were 100% rented and all rents are paid in full. It also includes other revenue such as laundry or parking income. |
| PP | Purchase Price: (PP=NOI/CAP) |
| PPF | Price Per Foot (PPF=Sales Price/Rentable Square Footage) |
| PPU | Price Per Unit: (PPU=Sales Price/# Units) |
| PSA | Purchase and Sales Agreement |
| ROE | Return-On-Equity is a calculation based on end-of-year performance. Factored into this is the increase in property value; reduction in principal balance. Cash Flow ROE=Annual Cash Flow/Equity |
| ROI | Return On Investment - Used to measure the performance and evaluate the efficiency of an investment. |
| TO | Turnover (stable properties have minimal turnover) _% annual turnover rate =Move outs/total # units |
| | |

## COMMONLY USED WORD AND PHRASES

| Word or Phrase | Meaning |
|---|---|
| Ad Valorem | An assessment of taxes against a property according to its value. |
| Borrowers | Individuals, revocable trusts and LLCs. |
| Experience | Borrowers must have current or recent income property ownership. |
| Full Recourse | The Borrowers must sign personally for the loan. |
| Impounds | The Lender will escrow taxes and insurance. |
| Income | There are three types of income:<br>**Earned or Ordinary income** - derived from the hours you exchange at your job for financial compensation (wages or salaries).<br>**Portfolio or Tax Free** - interest income on bank deposits, dividends, or capital gains. This income group includes tax-free income (not an increase of wealth) such as municipal and state bonds.<br>**Passive or Capital Gain** – Capital gain results from the sale or exchange of assets used in a trade or business or held for investment. Passive income is derived from the ownership of rental property, author's royalties, and income generated from owning patents or license agreements. |
| Net Worth | The borrowers must have a net worth equal to or greater than the loan amount. |
| Nonrecourse Debt | This type of financing does not require the Borrower to assume personal liability for the loan. If the Borrower defaults on the loan, the Lender can take ownership of the property in a foreclosure proceeding, but the Lender is limited only to the value of the collateral (property). |
| Post Close Liquidity | The borrowers must have post-closing cash of at least 5 percent of the loan amount. |
| Rate Caps | The interest rate charge cannot change more than a specified amount during the life of the loan. |
| Seasoning | A period of 1-12 months. Refinances are generally not considered during the first 12 months. |

# APPENDIX D

## LIFE EXPECTANCY OF KEY BUILDING COMPONENTS

All of the components that make the investment property what it is should be studied and a table similar to the one shown below should be prepared. In doing so the life expectancy of these components will be ascertained and provision for replacement and or upgrading can be made.

## Site and Landscaping

| Site and Landscaping | Years | Year Built / Installed | Comment |
| --- | --- | --- | --- |
| Asphalt Driveway | 15-20 | | |
| Asphalt with Acrylic Coating or Cushion | 12-15 | | |
| Brick and Concrete Patios | 15-25 | | |
| Concrete Walk | 40-50 | | |
| Gravel Walks | 4-6 | | |
| Polyvinyl Fences | 100+ | | |
| Sprinkler Heads | 10-15 | | |
| Underground PVC Piping | 60+ | | |
| | | | |
| | | | |
| | | | |
| | | | |

## Site Pool

| Swimming Pool | Years | Year Built / Installed | Comment |
| --- | --- | --- | --- |
| Swimming Pool Decking | 15 | | |
| Swimming Pool Tiles | 10 | | |
| Swimming Pool Walls and Foundation | 25+ | | |
| Swimming Pool Equipment | 7-10 | | |

## Building Foundation

Properly mixed, poured and laid concrete footings and foundations will last a lifetime. Concrete block as a foundation will last a lifetime.

| Footings and Foundations | Years | Year Built / Installed | Comment |
|---|---|---|---|
| Poured Footings and Foundations | 100+ | | |
| Concrete Block | 100+ | | |

## Framing

| Structural Framing | Years | Year Built / Installed | Comment |
|---|---|---|---|
| Poured Concrete Systems | 100+ | | |
| Structural Insulated Panels | 100+ | | |
| Wood Framed | 100+ | | |
| Wall Panels, Roof and Floor Trusses | 30+ | | |
| Hardboard, soft-wood, plywood OSB and particleboard | 60+ | | |
| Engineered Lumber Laminated Strand Lumber | 100+ | | |
| Laminated Veneer Lumber | 80+ | | |
| Trusses | 100+ | | |

## Building Exterior

Masonry is one of the most enduring exterior building components. Fireplaces, chimneys, and brick veneers can last the lifetime of a home.

| Masonry and Concrete | Years | Year Built / Installed | Comment |
|---|---|---|---|
| Brick | 100+ | | |
| Stone | 100+ | | |
| Veneer | 100+ | | |
| Sealer Caulking | 2-20 | | |

## Siding and Accessories

| Siding and Accessories | Years | Year Built / Installed | Comment |
|---|---|---|---|
| Aluminum Downspouts | 30 | | |
| Aluminum Gutters | 20 | | |
| Aluminum Shutters | 20 | | |
| Brick | 100+ | | |
| Galvanized Steel Gutters / Downspouts | 20 | | |
| Manufactured Stone | 100+ | | |
| Soffits / Facias | 50 | | |
| Stone | 100+ | | |
| Stucco | 50-100 | | |
| Trim | 25 | | |
| Vinyl | 100+ | | |
| Wood Shutters | 20 | | |

## Outside Door (entry), Windows and Skylights

| Doors, Windows and Skylights | Years | Year Built / Installed | Comment |
|---|---|---|---|
| Fiberglass Door | 100+ | | |
| Fire-Rated Steel Door | 100+ | | |
| Screen Door | 40 | | |
| Vinyl Door | 20 | | |
| Wood Door | 100+ | | |
| | | | |
| Aluminum Windows and Skylights | 15-20 | | |
| Vinyl Windows | 20-40 | | |
| Wood Windows | 30+ | | |
| | | | |

## Outside Paint

Surface preparation is the most important factor in determining paint life.

| Paint | Years | Year Built / Installed | Comment |
|-------|-------|------------------------|---------|
| Paint | 15+ | | |

## Interior Door

| Door | Years | Year Built / Installed | Comment |
|------|-------|------------------------|---------|
| Closet | 100+ | | |
| French | 30-50 | | |
| Wood (hollow core) | 20-30 | | |
| Wood (solid core) | 30-100+ | | |

## Floors

| Floors | Years | Year Built / Installed | Comment |
|--------|-------|------------------------|---------|
| Bamboo | 100+ | | |
| Brick Pavers | 100+ | | |
| Carpet | 8-10 | | |
| Concrete | 50+ | | |
| Engineered Wood | 50+ | | |
| Exotic Wood | 100+ | | |
| Granite | 100+ | | |
| Laminate | 15-25 | | |
| Linoleum | 25 | | |
| Marble | 100+ | | |
| Slate | 100 | | |
| Terrazzo | 75+ | | |
| Tile | 75-100 | | |
| Vinyl | 25 | | |

## Cabinetry and Storage Units

| Cabinets and Storage Units | Years | Year Built / Installed | Comment |
|---|---|---|---|
| Bath Room Cabinets | 100+ | | |
| Closet Shelves | 100+ | | |
| Laundry Cabinets | 100+ | | |
| Kitchen Cabinets | 50 | | |

## Ceilings, Walls and Finishes

| Ceilings, Walls and Finishes | Years | Year Built / Installed | Comment |
|---|---|---|---|
| Acoustical Ceilings | 100+ | | |
| Ceiling Suspension | 100+ | | |
| Ceramic Tile | 100+ | | |
| Standard Gypsum | 100+ | | |
| Paint | 12+ | | |

## Fixtures and Faucets

| Fixtures and Faucets | Years | Year Built / Installed | Comment |
|---|---|---|---|
| Acrylic Kitchen Sinks | 50 | | |
| Cast Iron Bathtub | 50 | | |
| Enamel Steel Kitchen Sinks | 5-10 | | |
| Faucets | 15-20 | | |
| Fiberglass Bathtubs and Showers | 10-15 | | |
| Saunas / Steam Rooms | 15-20 | | |
| Shower Enclosures / Modules | 50 | | |
| Shower Heads | 100+ | | |
| Shower Door | 25 | | |
| Stainless Steel Kitchen Sinks | 50 | | |
| Toilets / Bidets | 50 | | |
| Whirlpool Tubs | 20-40 | | |

## HVAC Equipment

Heating, ventilation and air-conditioning systems require regular maintenance to work properly. Due to the constant advances in equipment design, associated operating cost are reduced and may offset the installation of new equipment.

| HVAC Equipment | Years | Year Built / Installed | Comment |
|---|---|---|---|
| Air Conditioners | 10-15 | | |
| Air Quality System | 15 | | |
| Attic Fans | 15-25 | | |
| Boilers | 20-35 | | |
| Central Air Conditioning Units | 12-15 | | |
| Electric Dampers | 20+ | | |
| Dehumidifiers | 8 | | |
| Diffusers, Grilles and Registers | 25 | | |
| Duct | 10 | | |
| DX Water or Steam | 20 | | |
| Electric Radiant Heater | 40 | | |
| Furnace | 15-20 | | |
| Heat Exchangers (shell + tube) | 10-15 | | |
| Heat Pumps | 15 | | |
| Heat Recovery Ventilators | 20 | | |
| Hot Water or Steam Radiant Heater | 40 | | |
| Induction and Fan-Coil Units | 10-15 | | |
| Molded Insulation | 100+ | | |
| Shell and Tube | 20 | | |
| Thermostats | 25 | | |
| Ventilators | 7-10 | | |
| Water Heaters | 20+ | | |

## Appliances

Appliances have a longer life than their usefulness. Newer models are more efficient and require less energy to operate.

| Appliances | Years | Year Built / Installed | Comment |
|---|---|---|---|
| Air Conditioners (wall and window) | 8-15 | | |
| Compactors | 6 | | |
| Dishwashers | 9 | | |
| Dryers (cloths) | 10 | | |
| Exhaust Fans | 10 | | |
| Freezers | 10-20 | | |
| Gas Ovens | 10-18 | | |
| Microwave ovens | 9 | | |
| Range / Oven Hoods | 12-15 | | |
| Ranges (electric) | 13-15 | | |
| Ranges (gas) | 15-17 | | |
| Refrigerators | 9-13 | | |
| Washing Machine | 5-15 | | |

## Miscellaneous

| | Years | Year Built / Installed | Comment |
|---|---|---|---|
| Garage Doors | 20-25 | | |
| Garage Door Openers | 10-15 | | |
| Security Systems | 5-10 | | |
| Smoke Heat Detectors | 7-10 | | |
| Carbon Monoxide Detectors | 7-10 | | |
| Lighting Fixtures | 100 | | |
| Lighting Controls | 10+ | | |

# APPENDIX E

## RESOURCES

## ABSTRACTORS

| | |
|---|---|
| Long Island, NY | **Abstracts, Incorporated**<br>585 Steward Avenue<br>Garden City, NY 11530<br>(516) 683-1000<br>E-mail: info@AbstractsInc.com |
| | \*\*\* |
| Ohio | **Abstractor Services Inc.**<br>3195 Dayton Xenia Road<br>Suite 900-397<br>Beavercreek, OH 45434<br>(937) 675-2700<br>http://www.AbstractorServices.com |
| | \*\*\* |
| Nationwide | **American Document & Title LLC**<br>1300 Whitacre Dive<br>Clearwater, FL 33764<br>(727) 412-8010<br>http://www.AmeriDocsTitleSearch.com |
| | \*\*\* |
| Connecticut, Maine, New Hampshire, and Rhode Island | **ASK Land Title Services, LLC**<br>38 Fieldstone Lane<br>Candia, NH 03034<br>(603) 483-1039<br>http://www.AskTitleServices.com<br>Email: Title.Orders@ASKTitleServices.com |
| | \*\*\* |
| All of Florida, Georgia, Maryland, Ohio, and Massachusetts<br>Limited coverage in Alabama, Arizona, Illinois, Kentucky, Michigan, Missouri, Nevada, New Jersey, New Mexico, New York, Pennsylvania, and Washington | **Easy Title Search**<br>7950 S. Military Trail<br>Suite 102<br>Lake Worth, FL 33463<br>(855) 888-4853<br>http://www.EasyTitleSearch.com |
| | \*\*\* |
| Florida | **FastTitleSearch.com, LLC**<br>http://www.FastTitleSearch.com<br>E-mail: support@FastTitleSearch.com |
| | \*\*\* |
| Florida | **Florida Title Search**<br>http://www.FloridaTitleSearch.com |

\*\*\*

| | |
|---|---|
| Nationwide | **Nationwide Abstractor Services**<br>2100 US-19 Alt.<br>Palm Harbor, FL 34683<br>(800) 346-9152<br>http://www.NationwideTitleClearing.com |
| | \*\*\* |
| Oklahoma | **Oklahoma Abstractor's Directory**<br>http://www.ok.gov/abstractor/Abstractor_Director<br>y |
| | \*\*\* |
| New York State | **Orange Abstractor Services**<br>222 Greenwich Avenue<br>Goshen, NY 10924<br>(845) 294-3331 |
| | \*\*\* |
| Metro New York, Long Island, and Mid-Hudson New York | **Partners Abstract Corp.**<br>1025 Old Country Road #409<br>Westbury, NY 11590<br>(516) 338-2655<br>E-mail: bobby@PartnersAbstract.com |
| | \*\*\* |
| Nationwide | **Pro Title USA**<br>Multiple offices across the United States<br>Headquarters: Holland, PA<br>(888) 878-8081<br>http://www.ProTitleUSA.com<br>E-mail: info@ProTitleUSA.com |
| | \*\*\* |
| Delaware, Maryland, New Jersey, New York, Pennsylvania, and Washington, DC | **REO America Abstract Inc.**<br>123 S. Broad Street<br>Suite 1225<br>Philadelphia, PA 19109<br>(215) 320-5770<br>http://www.REOAmericaAbstract.com |
| | \*\*\* |
| Arkansas, Kentucky, North Carolina, South Carolina, Tennessee, and Virginia | **Title Searcher**<br>(866) 604-3674<br>http://www.TitleSearcher.com |
| | \*\*\* |
| Nationwide | **US Title Records**<br>160 Greentree Drive<br>Suite 101<br>Dover, DE 19904<br>Fax: (302) 269-3942<br>http://www.USTitleRecords.com<br>E-mail: Office@USTitleRecords.com |

\*\*\*

**Vital Abstract LLC**

3700 Route 27
Suite 102B
New Jersey                Princeton, NJ 08540
(732) 230-2574
http://www.VitalAbstract.com
E-mail: sales@VitalAbstract.com

\*\*\*

## APARTMENTS

**Apartment Rent Search**

www.apartments.com

\*\*\*

**Apartments for Rent**

www.forrent.com

\*\*\*

**My New Place**

www.MyNewPlace.com

\*\*\*

## APARTMENT ORGANIZATIONS

**Commercial Real Estate Exchange**

(512) 346-9158
http://commrex

\*\*\*

**Institute of Real Estate Management (IREM)**

430 N. Michigan Avenue
Chicago, Illinois 60611
(800) 837-0706
www.IREM.org

\*\*\*

**The Landlord Protection Agency**

(877) 984-3572
www.thelpa.com

\*\*\*

**National Apartment Association (NAA)**

201 N. Union Street, Suite 200
Alexandria, Virginia 22314
(703) 518-6141
www.naahq.org

\*\*\*

**National Association of Real Estate Investors**

10400W. Overland Road #232
Boise, Idaho 83709-1449
(208) 89-SMILE
www.narei

\*\*\*

**National Multi-Housing Council (NMHC)**
1850 M Street NW, Suite 540
Washington, D.C. 20036-5803
(202) 974-2300
www.NMHC.org

\*\*\*

**National Real Estate Investor**
www.nreionline.com

\*\*\*

## APPRAISERS

**National Association of Real Estate Appraisers**
World Headquarters
(760) 327-5284
info@narea-assoc.org

\*\*\*

**Nationwide Property and Appraisal Services, LLC**
**10 Foster Avenue, Suite C3**
**Gibbsboro, New Jersey 08026**
Telephone: 856-258-6977
FAX: 856-385-7065
E-mail: appraisals@onestopappraisals.com

\*\*\*

## COMPARABLE SALES

**LoopNet**
101 California Street
San Francisco, CA  94111
(415) 243-4200
www.loopnet.com

\*\*\*

**Costar Research**
www.costar.com

\*\*\*

**Commercial Listings**
www.CIMLS.com

\*\*\*

**Commrex**
**Real Capital Analytics**
www.rcanalyttics.com

\*\*\*

**REI, Inc.**
www.reis.com

\*\*\*

**Reis Reports**
(800) 366-7347
www.reis.com

\*\*\*

## ENVIRONMENTAL

### Environmental Data Resources Corp.
www.edrnet.com

\*\*\*

## ESA and PCA INSPECTION COMPANIES

### ATC Associates
www.atcassociates.com

\*\*\*

### Criterium Engineers
www.criterium_commercial.com

\*\*\*

### Terracon
www.terreaon.com

\*\*\*

## GENERAL

### Constant Contact, Inc.
E-mail Marketing
(866) 876-8464
www.constantcontact.com

## GOVERNMENT

### US Bureau of the Census
### New York Regional Office
32 Old Slip, 9th Floor
New York, NY, 10005
(212) 584-3402
www.census.gov/regions

\*\*\*

### Bureau of Labor Statistics
www.bls.gov
www.factfinder.census.gov

\*\*\*

## GOVERNMENT SALES

### FDIC Real Estate Sales
http://fdic.gov/buying/owned/index.html

\*\*\*

### IRS Auction
http://www.treasury.gov/auctions/irs/

\*\*\*

### US Marshals Services
### Asset Forfeiture Sales
http://www.justice.gov/marshals

\*\*\*

### CWS Asset Management and Sales
http://www.cwsmarketing.com/ustd_realestate.htm

\*\*\*

**Chronos Solutions**
http://www.chronossolutions.com/properties/us-marshals-service-properties
***

**Bid4Assets**
http://www.bid4assets.com/storefront/?sfid=150
***

**USDA Properties for Sale**
http://www.resales.usda.gov/
***

## HOME VALUES

**National Association of Realtors**
www.realtor.com
***

**Trulia**
www.trulia.com
***

**Zillows**
**www.zillow.com**
***

## INFORMATION SERVICES

**Advantage Tenant**
(800) 894-9047
www.AdvantageTenant.com
***

**Citi Credit Bureau**
(800) 710-2484
www.citicredit.net
***

**Free Advice**
www.FreeAdvice.com
***

**Legal Zoom**
(800) 773-0888
www.LegalZoom.com
***

**The National Landlord Tenant Guides**
www.RentLaw.com
***

**Tenant Alert**
(866) 272-8400
www.tenantalert.com
***

**Tenant Verify**
www.tenantverify
***

**Validus Information Services**
www.ValidUSInfo.com
\*\*\*

**You Check Credit.com**
www.youcheckcredit.com
\*\*\*

## INVESTOR ASSOCIATIONS

**National Association of Real Estate Investors**
235 Peachtree NE, Suite 400
Atlanta, Georgia 30303
(877) 545-9975
http://www.narei.com
\*\*\*

**National Real Estate Investor**
http://www.nreionline.com
\*\*\*

## LAUNDRY SERVICE COMPANIES

**Coinmach**
www.coinmach.com
\*\*\*

**Jetz Service Company**
www.jetzservice.com
\*\*\*

**Mac-Gray**
www.macgray.com
\*\*\*

## LEGAL SERVICES

**Legal Zoom**
https://www.legalzoom.com/attorneys/attorney-directory
\*\*\*

**Nationwide Legal LLC**
http://www.nationwideasap.com/management/
\*\*\*

## LENDERS

| | |
|---|---|
| Nationwide FHA Mortgagee and Multifamily Accelerated Processing (MAP) lender | **AGM Financial Services Inc**<br>20 South Charles Street, Suite 1000<br>Baltimore, MD 21201<br>(800) 729-4266<br>www.agmfinancial.com |

\*\*\*

| | |
|---|---|
| Commercial Mortgages | **Apple Bank for Savings**<br>1395 Northern Blvd.<br>Manhasset, NY 11030<br>(914) 902-2775<br>https://www.applebank.com/About/Get-In-Touch/Contact-Us |

***

| | |
|---|---|
| Debt capital for the purchase, refinance, and construction of commercial real estate properties. | **Arbor Commercial Mortgages LLC**<br>333 Earle Ovington Blvd, Suite 900<br>Uniondale, NY 11553<br>(800) 878-5160<br>www.thearbornet.com |

***

| | |
|---|---|
| Senior Housing/Healthcare Debt and Equity financing | **Cambridge Realty Capital**<br>125 South Wacker Drive, Suite 1800<br>Chicago, IL 60606<br>(312) 357-1601<br>www.cambridgecap.com |

***

| | |
|---|---|
| Commercial Mortgages | **David Cronheim Mortgage Company**<br>205 Main Street, Suite 101<br>Chatham, NJ 07928<br>www.cronheimmortgage.com |

***

| | |
|---|---|
| Debt Financing | **Cohen Financial**<br>Corporate Headquarters<br>227 West Monroe Street, Suite 1000<br>Chicago, IL 60606<br>(312) 346-5680<br>www.cohenfinancial.com |

***

| | |
|---|---|
| Permanent Debt for Refinance or Acquisition; Bridge Loans; Mezzanine Debt; Discounted Pay-off Financing; Construction Debt; Joint Venture Equity; Tax Credit Advisory & Syndication. | **Conlon Capital**<br>401 W. Ontario Street, Suite 400<br>Chicago, IL 60654<br>(312) 521-5990<br>www.coloncapital.com |

***

| | |
|---|---|
| Debt Financing | **CW Financial Services**<br>One Charles River Place<br>63 Kendrick Street<br>Needham, MA 02494<br>(781) 707-9300<br>www.cwcapital.com |

***

| | |
|---|---|
| Commercial Mortgages | **Eastern Union Commercial**<br>info@easternuc.com |

***

| | |
|---|---|
| Financing for multi-family and healthcare facilities | **Great Lakes Financial Group**<br>1020 Huron Road, Suite 100<br>Cleveland, OH 44115<br>(216) 861-1300<br>www.glhousing.com |

***

| | |
|---|---|
| Commercial Mortgages | **Hunt Mortgage Group**<br>Corporate Headquarters<br>230 Park Avenue New York, NY 10169<br>(212) 317-5700<br>http://www.huntmortgagegroup.com/contact-us/ |

***

| | |
|---|---|
| Equity and debt financings, restructuring/workout advisory, land and investment sales, co-development ventures, and principal investments For: apartment, condominium, condo-hotel and mixed-use projects. | **Madison Capital Group**<br>800 Brickell Avenue, PH 3<br>Miami, FL 33131<br>(305) 375-9110<br>www.madisoncapitalgroup.com |

***

| | |
|---|---|
| Equity loans; mezzanine loans; construction loans and bridge loans. | **Meecorp Capital Markets LLC**<br>2050 Center Street, Suite 640<br>Fort Lee, NJ 07024<br>(201) 944-9330<br>principal@meecorp.com |

***

| | |
|---|---|
| Bridge Lender for: Multifamily; Hospitality; Retail; Industrial; Office; Mixed Use; Land | **Mercury Capital**<br>380 Lexington Avenue, Suite 1721<br>New York, NY 10168<br>(212) 661-8700<br>info@mercurycapital.com |

***

| | |
|---|---|
| Commercial Mortgages | **Meridian Capital Group**<br>1 Battery Park Plaza<br>New York, NY 10004<br>(212) 972-3600<br>www.meridiancapital.com |

***

| | |
|---|---|
| Nationwide Financing for commercial properties, including multifamily, healthcare facilities, office, industrial, retail, and student, senior, and military housing. | **M&T Realty Capital Corp.**<br>25 S. Charles Street<br>Baltimore, MD21201<br>(410) 545-2411<br>https://www.mandtrealtycapital.com/Contact_Us/<br>contactus.html |

\*\*\*

| | |
|---|---|
| Bridge loans | **Mountain Funding LLC**<br>13860 Ballantyne Corp. Place, Suite 130<br>Charlotte, NC 28277<br>www.mountainfunding.com |

\*\*\*

| | |
|---|---|
| Nationwide mortgage lender. | **Primary Capital Advisors**<br>2060 Mt. Paran Road NW, Suite 101<br>Atlanta, GA 30327<br>(404 365-9300<br>www.primarycapital.com |

\*\*\*

| | |
|---|---|
| Financial services in the multifamily, affordable and seniors housing and health care markets. | **Red Capital Group**<br>10 West Broad Street<br>Columbus, OH 43215<br>(800) 837-5100<br>www.redcapital group.com |

\*\*\*

| | |
|---|---|
| Commercial Mortgages | **Walker & Dunlop**<br>7501 Wisconsin Avenue<br>Bethesda, MD 20814<br>(301) 215-5555<br>https://www.walkerdunlop.com/Pages/default.asp |

\*\*\*

| | |
|---|---|
| Commercial Mortgages | **Wells Fargo Multifamily Capital**<br>2010 Corporate Ridge, Suite 1000<br>McLean, VA 22102<br>(877) 734-5592<br>www.wellsfargo.com/wfcm |

\*\*\*

## NATIONWIDE HARD MONEY LENDERS

**Lending Home**
(800) 215-9222
http://www.lendinghome.com

\*\*\*

**Lima One Capital**
201 E. McBee Avenue, Suite 300
Greenville, SC  29601

(800) 390-4212
http://www.limaonecapital.com

\*\*\*

**RCN Capital**
(860) 432-5858
info@RCNCapital.com

\*\*\*

CPSIA information can be obtained
at www.ICGtesting.com
Printed in the USA
LVHW011821291219
641984LV00022B/1688